Biological Clocks in Marine Organisms

Biological Clocks in Marine Organisms:
The Control of Physiological and Behavioral Tidal Rhythms

JOHN D. PALMER
Professor of Biological Sciences
New York University

A Wiley-Interscience Publication
JOHN WILEY & SONS
New York · London · Sydney · Toronto

Library of Congress Cataloging in Publication Data:

Palmer, John D   1932-
  Biological clocks in marine organisms.

  "A Wiley-Interscience publication."
  Includes bibliographies.
  1. Marine fauna.   2. Biology—Periodicity.
I. Title.   [DNLM: 1. Biological clocks.   2. Marine
biology.   QH90 P174b 1974]

QL121.P34   591.1   74-917
ISBN 0-471-65768-9

Printed in the United States of America

10 9 8 7 6 5 4 3 2 1

To Johnny

Preface

This book is about bioclock-controlled tidal rhythms, that is, bimodal organismic oscillations with periods of approximately 24.8 h, which will persist in constant conditions in the laboratory. An attempt has been made to write for people in and outside of the field of biochronometry and for those who do and do not work on tidal organisms. Disregarding the impossibility of such an all-level presentation (but leaving the stated intent here as a foothold for reviewers), I have assembled the present volume.

The book is intended to be a compilation and distillation of the best literature on the subject of tidal rhythms and therefore is to stand as a reference repository. It is also an attempt to synthesize an undisciplined literature into a few generalizations pointing the direction toward future work.

The organization is straightforward: In an attempt to provide for the reader a certain familiarity with the basic subject matter the early chapters survey known rhythms; then follows a segment describing experiments with tidal rhythms and the properties derived from these laboratory manipulations; and finally, the last segment uses some of these properties —and also those of circadian rhythms—to draw a rough sketch of the clockworks underlying persistent rhythms. Some readers may question the organizational philosophy of the first section, but I decided only after considerable thought—no doubt being prejudiced as a physiologist—on an arrangement by function. This choice tends to underemphasize those very interesting and experimentally useful organisms that are known to display simultaneous rhythms in many physiological and behavioral processes. I have tried to compensate for this by cross-referencing and by occasional digressions into syntheses for specific species. I hope this will be adequate.

Because of the diverse backgrounds of the intended audience, many of the organisms will be unfamiliar to some readers. Therefore, pictures of those receiving widest coverage, and a smattering of the natural history of most, are included for didactic reasons and to provide a better perspective of what the rhythms mean to the organisms. Also, the methods and tools of biochronometrists often differ from conventional laboratory procedures, so descriptions and figures of some homemade apparatuses appear in the text. Terms peculiar to chronobiology are defined when first used and then compiled into a glossary. Finally, at the end of each major chapter, I have included a "summary and conclusions" section to compensate for inadvertant exponibles in the main text.

I wish to thank all those who have helped in the preparation of the manuscript, especially my students Miss Carol Hayes and Mrs. Judith Goodenough, and Professors Marguerite Webb and Frank A. Brown for endless hours of discussion and critical reviews of all parts of the book. I also acknowledge the Cambridge Philosophical Society, and especially Professor E. N. Willmer, for permission to expand my review article into this book and for the invaluable help they provided in the production of that article.

John D. Palmer

November 1973

Contents

Biological Clocks in Marine Organisms

1 Introduction

There are many rhythmic physiological, biochemical, electrochemical, and behavioral aspects of organismic life. These range in frequency from spike output by the nervous system, through heartbeat, to daily cycles, to 54-yr tree-ring cycles, and so on. Some of these rhythms, the few that approximately match the prominent geophysical cycles on earth, are unique in several fascinating ways. They share such properties as (1) persistence when isolated from entraining cycles in the environment, (2) a period length virtually temperature-independent and immune to alteration by a great host of chemical substances, and (3) a phase that can be reset to any desired time. These rhythms have periods approximating a year (Figure 1-1), a synodic month (29.5 days) (Figure 1-2), a lunar

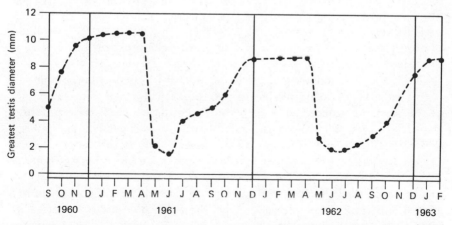

Figure 1-1. Annual rhythm in average testis size of 10 finches *(Quelea quelea)* during a 2.5-yr laboratory study. The birds were maintained at 22°C, under cycles of 12 h of light alternating with 12 h of darkness. At monthly intervals they were laparotomized, the left testis was measured, and the incision was closed (Lofts, 1964).

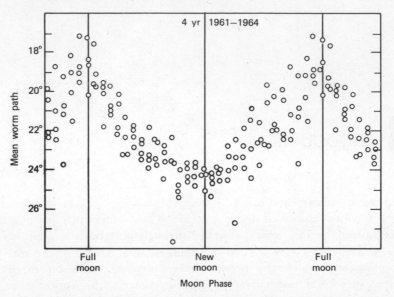

Figure 1-2. Monthly rhythm in orientation (away from two light sources) of planaria *(Dugesia dorotocephala)*. Other than during the test times, the worms were maintained in constant darkness and temperature. Each point represents the average path of 45 worm runs. The study encompasses 4 yr (Brown, 1969).

day (24.8 h), a solar day (Figure 1-3), and a tidal interval (12.4 h) (Figure 1-4). Because the rhythms will persist in the laboratory, where the major entraining environmental cycles are precluded, it is postulated that they are under the control of a timing mechanism within the organism called the *biological clock*.

The mode of functioning of the clock mechanism is thus far completely unknown, but analogue models and hypothetical schemes are rife. All of these can be reduced so as to fit into one of two clock conceptualizations (Chapter 10): the escapement and nonescapement hypotheses (Palmer, 1970; Brown, Hastings, and Palmer, 1970). Both concede the existence of some type of horologe within the organism but differ antipodally as to the means by which each produces its constant interval. The escapement-type of clock is capable of generating its own period autonomously and of functioning completely independently of the environment. This type of clock is analogous to a wristwatch or grandfather clock. In the organism it is thought to be a biochemical or biophysiochemical entity, probably existing at the cellular level, and capable of surviving replication during cell division without losing time. The nonescapement clock is more of a signaling mechanism, as are the sundial and the electric clock,

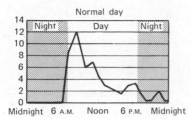

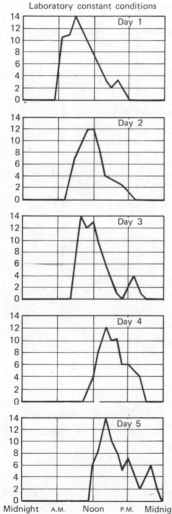

Figure 1-3. Daily rhythm in perch-hopping of a caged robin (*Turdus migratorius*). On day 1 the bird had been moved to constant dim light (<2 ft-c) and 20°C. Under these constant conditions the activity rhythm became slightly longer than 25 h (Palmer, 1966).

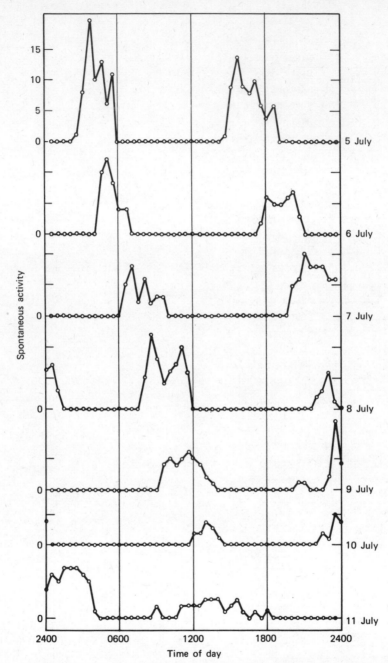

Figure 1-4. Tidal locomotor rhythm in a fiddler crab (*Uca pugnax*) maintained in constant darkness and 20°C. Ordinate values represent actograph movements per half hour. The peaks for the first few days are approximately centered on the times of low tide at the site of collection (Palmer, 1973).

which simply display the timing information they receive from the sun's movement and the alternating current from the power company. In the organism, this clock receives its timing information from an as yet unidentified geophysical force, one able to penetrate the barriers of standard laboratory constant conditions and organismic structure, into the intracellular milieu where the clock is located. The force must manifest some transferable information on periods of 24 and 24.8 h, and 29.5 and 365 days, for the nonescapement clock to "signal" to organismic physiology. Most of the known highly penetrating forces such as geomagnetism and background radiation do display intensity changes with the necessary frequencies, the periodicities being caused by the rotation of the earth on its axis in relation to the sun and moon. To date, neither hypothetical mechanism has accumulated sufficient supporting evidence to establish it as the actual one.

This book will focus mainly on tidal rhythms, but to set the stage, we will digress for a brief discussion of solar-day rhythms, a subject that has received the greatest attention by investigators working on clock-conrolled rhythms (for recent reviews, see Bünning, 1967; Sweeney, 1969; Brown et al., 1970; and Menaker, 1971). In nature these rhythms are precisely 24 h in length, but if they persist when the organism is brought into the lab and placed in continuous light of a constant intensity (LL in shorthand notation) or continuous darkness (DD) at a constant temperature (TT) (or when at least these two environmental parameters are held constant, the notation is CC for "constant conditions"), the period often differs somewhat from 24 h (Figure 1-5). A little over a decade ago this difference had such a profound significance to those workers concerned with the fundamental clockworks of the living horologe that the appellation *circadian* (from Latin circa, "about" and *diem,* "day") was given this property "to denote daily periods which may differ from 24 hours by not more than a few hours" (Halberg, Halberg, Barnum, and Bittner, 1959). The use of *may* in the definition permits the inclusion of exact 24-h periods also, but the term was obviously coined to stress the periods that differ from this value, for without them the word would not exist. Equally obvious, the term referred only to clock-controlled rhythms that persisted in CC, since only in CC is the period different from exactly 24 h. Twenty-four-hour rhythms that do not persist in CC belong not in the circadian classification but instead in the realm of ecology, since these "rhythms" are controlled directly by the environment, usually by the day–night oscillation in light intensity. However, the term quickly became used in the literature (by investigators apparently unaware of the true meaning and significance) in descriptions of any 24-h organismic rhythm they observed in the lab, field,

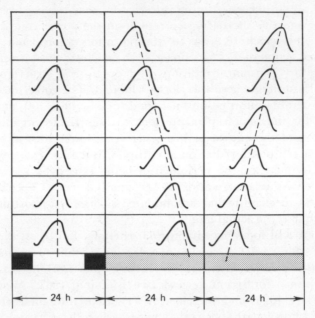

Figure 1-5. Diagram showing that in natural day–night cycles (first column: blackened portions of subtending block, signifying hours of darkness), the period of a solar-day rhythm is strictly 24 h. In laboratory constant conditions (second two columns: constant light intensity signified by gray blocks) the period can become longer or shorter than 24 h; that is, its *circadian* nature is revealed (Palmer, 1970).

or hospital ward, without ever testing its persistence in CC. Criticism of this usage was voiced (Palmer, 1964; Wurtman, 1967) but went unheeded.

After a time the lab in which the term *circadian* originated changed the definition "to include all such periods approximating 24 hours, with exact 24 hour periodicity as a special case" (Bartter, Delea, and Halberg, 1962). This change, whether intended or not, destroyed all remnants of the term's relative meaning and much of its original usefulness and gave it to the scientific world as a neologism synonymous with *daily or thereabouts,* thus justifying previous misusage by the uninitiated. However, in addition to having this new denotation, the term connotes, to some of us, a rhythm distinct from the majority of other biorhythms in that it matches a geophysical period, one that is clock-controlled and, more important, that signifies the property of period lability of the rhythm in CC. Thus, other organismic rhythms such as tidal, monthly, and annual rhythms, which differ slightly from their exact geophysical counterparts in CC, are referred to broadly as circatidal, circamonthly, and circannual.

To add to the confusion surrounding the meaning of *circadian,* there is a single frequency—24.8 h, the interval of a lunar day and the period of many organismic rhythms in the natural environment—that is found well within the upper range of circadian periods. I emphasize here that rhythms with this period are distinct in several ways from neighboring circadian frequencies. These differences (and similarities) make up much of the subject matter of this book.

The earth rotates on its axis once every 24 h and 51 min in relation to the moon (Figure 1-6). This duration (i.e., from moonrise to moonrise) is a lunar day, and within this time span, on most coasts of the world, two tidal inundations occur approximately 12.4 h apart. It is the moon's gravitational attraction that causes the oceans to "pile up" simultaneously into these tidal fronts, one bulge following under the overhead transit of the moon and the other directly opposite it on the other side of the earth. The moon, during its monthly journey around the earth, varies in declination between 28° 30′ north latitude and 28° 30′ south latitude, and these deviations produce considerable alteration in the extent of inundation of a particular shoreline. For example, when the moon circles the earth over the equator, both tides on the same day are essentially of equal amplitude at any given latitude, but when the moon

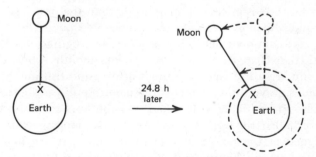

Figure 1-6. The relative movements of the moon and earth, which produce the lunar day. The earth rotates on its axis in a counterclockwise fashion, and the moon circles the earth in a similar direction. As the earth completes one rotation (24 h) relative to the sun, the moon's travels have placed it in a new location (therefore, it is not a stationary reference point). Thus, for a given longitude (signified above as X) to face the moon again, the earth must "catch up" by rotating an additional 13°. Consequently, the interval between successive moonrises at a given longitude is 24 h and 51 min.

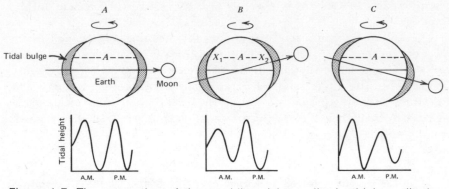

Figure 1-7. The generation of the semidiurnal inequality in tidal amplitude. During the span of one month, the moon's declination varies up to a maximum of 28½° north and south of the equator. When the moon is on the equator (as it is twice each month), both tides during a lunar day at a particular latitude (A) are equal in amplitude (Condition A). When the moon is north of the equator (Condition B), the tidal bulge is greater in the northern hemisphere when the moon is overhead, but on the other side of the earth the maximum is in the southern hemisphere. At this time, at longitude, X_1, the shoreline at latitude A is inundated only by the edge of the tidal bulge and experiences a lower high tide than it does 12.4 h later when it is facing the moon (position X_2). The same semidiurnal inequality in tidal depth is created when the moon is south of the equator (Condition C).

is north or south of the equator, one tidal exchange each lunar day at a particular latitude is greater in magnitude than the other (Figure 1-7). This latter phenomenon is called the *semidiurnal inequality*.

The sun's gravitational field plays a lesser, but significant, role in the extent of tidal exchange. Twice each synodic month, when the earth, moon, and sun are all in line (the times of new and full moon), (Figure 1-8A), the sun's gravitation augments the moon's pull on the seas causing the high tides to be higher than usual and the lows to be lower. These extremes are called the *spring tides*. When the moon, earth, and sun become aligned as the points of a right triangle (at the first and last quarters of the moon) (Figure 1-8B), the gravitational forces of the moon and sun no longer pull together and the shorelines experience the smallest ranges of tidal exchange during the month. These are the *neap tides* (Figure 1-9).

This periodic ebb and flow of the tide imposes alternating extreme ecological stress on the intertidal biota and often molds their physiological and/or behavioral responses into tidal rhythms. Often these rhythms persist when the organisms are moved to the tideless confines

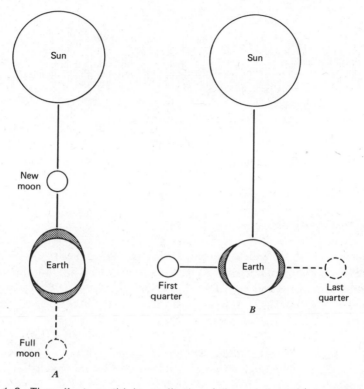

Figure 1-8. The effect on tidal amplitude of the relative movements of the moon, earth, and sun. A: When the three bodies are all in a line, the gravitational forces of the sun and moon augment each other causing the highest (spring) tides of the month. B: The gravitational forces of the moon and sun tend to counter each other when these two bodies form a right angle with the earth, and the tidal range is smallest at these times (neap tides).

of the laboratory (Figure 1-4), and the phase, at least initially, is synchronized with some point of the tidal cycle on the beach of collection (often high or low tide), the chosen phase being species-specific. Reducing the rhythmic response to its simplest descriptive dimension, it is traditionally referred to as a tidal rhythm. However, as will be pointed out later, this is probably an oversimplification: the rhythm should be described as a *bimodal* lunar-day rhythm, reflecting the period of an underlying 24.8-h lunar-day clock.

Reviews that include tidal rhythms have appeared in the past. Korringa (1947; 1957) discusses field studies, and lab work has been covered by Webb and Brown (1959), Fingerman (1960), Enright (1963), and Palmer (1973).

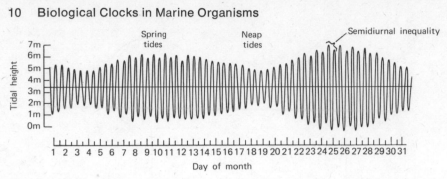

Figure 1-9. Semidiurnal inequality and fortnightly alteration in tidal exchange.

Literature Cited

Bartter, F. C., C. S. Delea, and F. Halberg. 1962. A map of blood and urinary changes related to circadian variations in adrenal cortical function in normal subjects. *Ann. N.Y. Acad. Sci.*, 98:969–983.

Brown, F. A., Jr. 1969. A hypothesis for extrinsic timing of circadian rhythms. *Can. J. Bot.*, 47:287–298.

Brown, F. A., Jr., . WJ. Hastings, and J. D. Palmer. 1970. *The Biological Clock: Two Views*, 2nd ed. Academic, New York.

Bünning, E. 1973. *The Physiological Clock*, 3rd ed. Springer-Verlag, New York.

Enright, J. T. 1963. Endogenous tidal and lunar rhythms. *Proc. XVI Inter. Cong. Zool.*, 4:355–359.

Fingerman, M. 1960. Tidal rhythmicity in marine organisms. *Cold Spring Harbor Symp. Quant. Biol.*, 25:481–489.

Halberg, F., E. Halberg, C. Barnum, and J. Bittner. 1959. Physiologic 24-hour periodicity in human beings and mice, the lighting regimen and daily routine. Ed., R. Withrow, *Photoperiodism and Related Phenomena in Plants and Animals. AAAS, Washington, D.C.*, pp. 803–873.

Korringa, P. 1947. Relations between the moon and periodicity in the breeding of marine animals. *Ecol. Monogr.*, 17:347–381.

Korringa, P. 1957. Lunar periodicity. In *Treatise on Marine Ecology and Palaeontology*, Vol. I. Waverly, Baltimore.

Lofts, B. 1964. Evidence of an autonomous reproductive rhythm in an equatorial bird *(Quelea quelea). Nature*, 201:523–524.

Menaker, M., Ed. 1971. *Biochronometry*. National Academy of Sciences, Washington, D.C.

Palmer, J. D. 1964. Circadian. *Science*, 145:296.

Palmer, J. D. 1966. How a bird tells the time of day. *Nat. Hist.*, 75:48–53.

Palmer, J. D. 1970. Introduction to biological clocks and rhythms. In J. Palmer, Ed. *The Biological Clock: Two Views.* Academic, New York, pp. 1–12.

Palmer, J. D. 1970. Biological clock. In P. Gray, Ed., *Encyclopedia of the Biological Sciences*, Van Nostrand Reinhold, New York, pp. 107–108.

Palmer, J. D. 1973. Tidal rhythms: the clock control of the rhythmic physiology of marine organisms. *Biol. Rev.*, 48:377–418.

Sweeney, B. M. 1969. *Rhythmic Phenomena in Plants*. Academic, New York.

Webb, H. M., and F. A. Brown, Jr. 1959. Timing long-cycle physiological rhythms. *Physiol. Rev.*, 39:127–161.

Wurtman, R. J. 1967. Ambiguities in the use of the term circadian. *Science*, 156:104.

2 Activity Rhythms

The fiddler crab, genus *Uca* (Figure 2-1), is an inhabitant of the intertidal zone of many coastlines. During both daytime and nighttime low tides, fiddler crabs emerge from their burrows to scurry around the exposed flats to feed, reconstruct burrows, court, and threaten one another. As the flood tide ascends the shoreline, they return to their burrows, often plug the entrance with a compact ball of substratum, and sit out the interval of inundation (Pearse, 1914; Schwartz and Safit, 1915; Hyman, 1920; Dembowski, 1926; and Barnwell, 1963, 1968).

The first tidal locomotor rhythm reported for a crab was found in *Uca pugnax*. Brown, Brown, Webb, Bennett, and Schriner (1956) and Bennett, Schriner, and Brown (1957) studied the spontaneous locomotor activity of *U. pugnax,* maintained individually in delicately balanced

Figure 2-1. The fiddler crab, *Uca pugnax.*

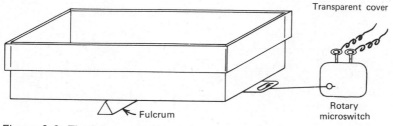

Transparent cover

Fulcrum

Rotary
microswitch

Figure 2-2. Tipping-pan actograph.

tipping actographs (Figure 2-2) in constant light and temperature and away from the direct influence of the tides. The crabs remained active under these conditions for only about 10 days, after which the entire laboratory population had to be changed. Individual responses were found to be variable, and the day-to-day precision of the rhythms decreased with time, so these investigators lumped the hourly data of 10 or 20 crabs together, and smoothed the resulting curves with a 3-h moving average. The population in CC displayed a clear cut tidal rhythm in activity with the bimodal rhythm peaking 50.1 ± 3.58 min later each day, and 3–5 h before the time of maximum low tide (Figure 2-3A).

By subjecting 29-day blocks of data to a standard statistical manipulation as described in Brown, Freeland, and Ralph (1955) and patterned after Chapman, and Bartel (1940), the tidal pattern of the locomotor activity was more-or-less randomized and no longer apparent in the data; the residual was then scrutinized and a low-amplitude (two-thirds that of the tidal) daily rhythm reported to be present (Figure 2-3B). The interval of major activity of this solar-day component occurred between 0600 and 1200 hours and its modulating effect on the tidal rhythm seen as higher maxima and minima in the morning than at other times of the day.

Enright (1963a), Aschoff (1965), and others have questioned the validity of the statistical analysis used above—adding a special caveat against the use of moving means, for this smoothing technique is known to sometimes create cycles in acyclic data. In offering such warnings they have provided a service to the biorhythm's community; they have also cast doubt on the reality of the rhythms in *Uca*. However, I, for one, have repeated the observations on *U. pugnax* and confirmed the earlier finding. In fact, when one records from hundreds of individual crabs, a certain small percentage are found to display especially precise rhythms. One such individual's persistent rhythm (in DD and 20°C) is portrayed in Figure 1-4 (Palmer, 1963, 1973). Using the interval between consecutive onsets of activity the average period of this rhythm is 12 h and 42 min. Using the interval between major peaks, a mean period of

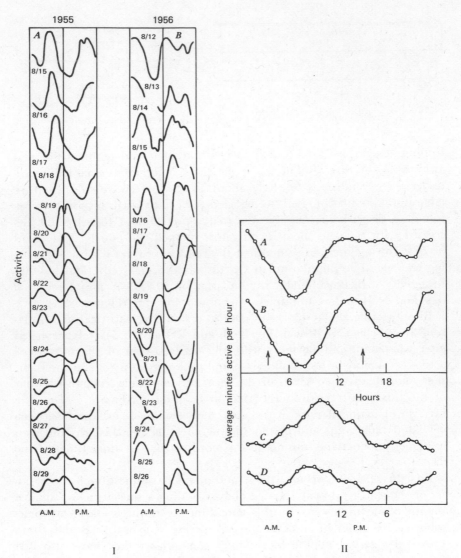

Figure 2-3. The spontaneous tidal locomotor activity of the fiddler crab (*Uca pugnax*) in LL (<2 ft-c) and ~22°C. (I) The average daily form of 10 crabs' locomotor pattern for two consecutive 15-day periods of observation. (II) Form-estimate curves for 29-day segments of data showing the tidal (curves *A* and *B*) and daily (*C* and *D*) components (Bennett, Shriner, and Brown, 1957).

12 h and 50 min is derived and, using the ends of activity bursts, 13 h and 2 min. Clearly, a circatidal rhythm is present. (En passant, it should be mentioned that the tides in nature over almost any short interval of days are also "circa"; For example, the average natural tidal period during the above observations was 12 h and 17 min.) Enright (1965) has reanalyzed the data of Bennett et al. (1957) using a spectrum analysis technique and has found that the bimodal period is really circatidal, being slightly longer than the tidal interval (Figure 2-4).

While I did not look for a mean-daily component along with the tidal

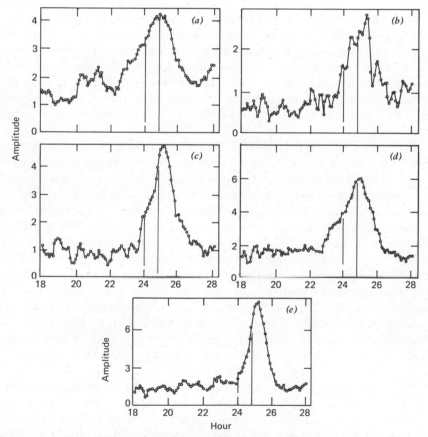

Figure 2.4. Periodogram analysis of sets of data collected by Bennett et al. (1957) (and used to construct some of the preceding figure). It can be seen that the major period in the data tends to be slightly longer than 24.8 h. No clear and separate peak appears at 24 h, but periodograms a–d are negatively skewed with mildly suggestive shoulders over 24 h (Enright, 1965).

one in *U. pugnax*, a priori one might be expected to exist, for the presence of a prominent circadian clock in this organism is well established. The latter controls daily rhythms in color change (Brown and Webb, 1948), oxygen consumption (Brown, Bennett, and Webb, 1954), phototaxis (Palmer, 1964), and sun-compass orientation (Herrnkind, 1968). Both tidal and daily components have been demonstrated (without extensive mathematical treatment) in the locomotory behavior of the penultimate-hour crab, *Sesarma reticulatum* (Palmer, 1967) (Figures 2-5, 2-6, 2-16) and the green crab, *Carcinus maenas* (Naylor, 1958) (Figure 2-14). However, in Enright's (1965) reanalysis of the data of Bennett et al. (1957), he reports the absence of any 24-h rhythm. Inspection of his periodograms (Figure 2-4) shows that four of five sets of data have broad peaks straddling hours 23.5 to 26; and all of these curves appear to be negatively skewed, with mildly suggestive shoulders at hour 24. In view of the accuracy of his analytic method (he had to use only moving averages, the only "raw" data published) and the fact that the claimed solar-day component is a low-amplitude one, I would suggest that the absence of a distinct peak at hour 24 in the periodogram is not surprising.

Barnwell (1966) improved on the maintenance of fiddler crabs in actographs and was thus able' to record tidal locomotor rhythms lasting nearly a month in LL in *individual U. pugnax* and *U. pugilator* [Atkinson and Naylor (1973) have confirmed Barnwell's finding with the latter species], and up to 46 days in *U. minax*. When he exposed the actographs to natural LD, the contained crabs displayed a quite precise 12.4-h rhythm (Figure 2-7). In LL (4 ft-c or less) the rhythm became circatidal; the period varied between individuals but was always slightly longer than 12.4 h (Figure 2-8) (the significance of this will be discussed in Chapter 10). Daily rhythmic components were also noted in his study. For example, in Figure 2-7, this is seen as an enhancement of tide-related activity for the first few hours after sunrise and sunset. In Figure 2-8, the diurnal component is much less obvious. After a period of time in LL some *U. minax* and *U. pugilator* individuals appeared to lose the tidal component of their activity pattern, while the circadian one was enhanced.

U. minax from the Mississippi bayous are subjected to only one tide per lunar day. In actographs in natural LD, only a diurnal rhythm was expressed. In a translocation experiment, several of these crabs were brought to Massachusetts and exposed in cages to the twice-a-day tides near Woods Hole for 26 days. On placement in DD, it was found that they all had acquired an east-coast tidal rhythm (Barnwell, 1968). *U. minax* from the alternating diurnal–semidiurnal tides of the California coast appear to display only diurnal rhythms in CC (Honegger, 1973).

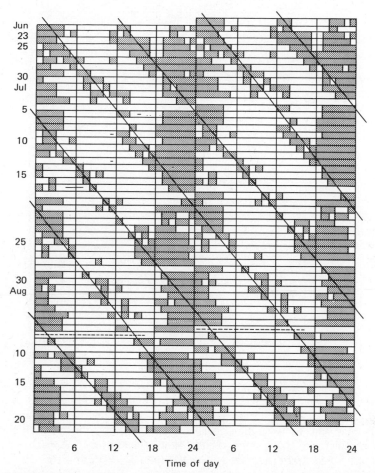

Figure 2-5. The mean daily and tidal components in the penultimate-hour crab (*Sesarma reticulatum*). Darkened areas signify the hours when the population average activity was higher than the daily mean. An obvious solar-day component is seen with peak activity falling approximately between the hours 7 PM and 4 AM. To visualize the movement of the tidal peaks across the solar day, the graph has been duplicated and the copy displaced upward by one day to the right of the original. Parallel oblique lines superimposed over the figure represent the midpoint of daily high tides. Dashed lines signify hours of mechanical failures of the recording system. The entire crab populations were replaced on July 5, 18, and 29 and August 10 (Palmer, 1967).

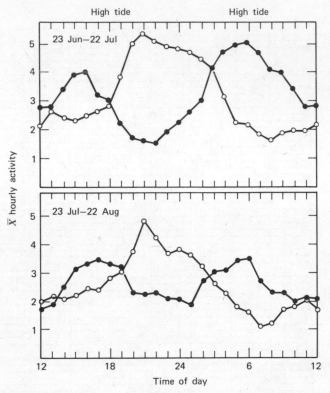

Figure 2-6. Form-estimate curves of the daily and tidal rhythmic components in the activity pattern of the penultimate-hour crab (*Sesarma reticulatum*) for two consecutive months. The mean solar-day rhythm is indicated by the open circles; the time scale on the abscissa is pertinent only for this rhythmic component. The solid circles represent the bimodal lunar-day rhythmic component; maxima in this rhythm correspond to the times of high tide (the midpoints of high tide are indicated at the top of the figure (Palmer, 1967).

Two species of Brazilian fiddler crabs, *U. maracoani* and *U. mordax,* have also been shown to have average group tidal rhythms in CC (Barn-well, 1963). In *U. mordax* a statistically "exposed" daily component, essentially equal in amplitude to the tidal component, was also present. To see what contribution these dual components actually made to the day-to-day variations in the locomotor pattern, Barnwell combined algebraically the mean solar- and lunar-day curves in the proper phase relationship (remember that the tidal cycle scans the day at a rate of 50 min/day) for each day of a fortnight and compared the resulting curves to the population average curves for that day (Figure 2-9). The agree-

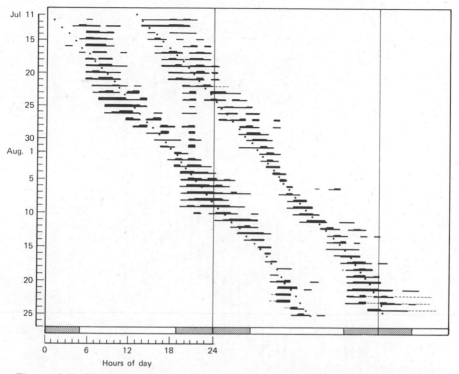

Figure 2-7. Rhythmic activity pattern of one male fiddler crab (*Uca minax*) in natural LD. The heights of the blocks indicate the percent of each hour during which the crab was active. The descending chain of dots indicates the predicted times of high tide at the beach of collection. Broken lines indicate failure of the recording system (modified from Barnwell, 1966).

ment between computed and recorded activity over a 14-day period was rather good, with a correlation coefficient of $+0.64$. This simple comparison did not take into account the 50% reduction in activity that occurred over the fortnight of incarceration, greatly reducing the agreement (the computed curve underestimating the activity level during the beginning of the comparison and overestimating it at the conclusion).

U. mordax living on the Caribbean shore of Costa Rica is subjected to only one tide per day and expresses only this frequency in actograph studies in the lab. Barnwell (1968) transplanted several of these animals to the opposite side of the 110-mile-wide continent and exposed them in a cage to the twice-per-lunar-day tides on the Pacific shore for 5 days. Transfer to actographs in DD then indicated that at least some had adopted the twice-daily tidal rhythm in this short time.

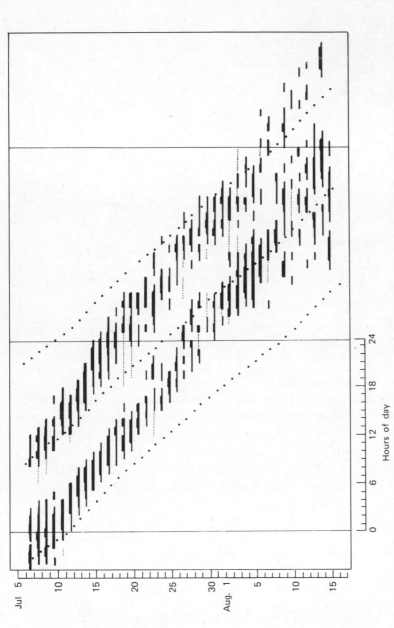

Figure 2-8. Rhythmic activity pattern of one male fiddler crab (*Uca minax*) in LL (<1ft-c). The heights of the blocks indicate the percent of each hour during which the crab was active. The descending chain of dots indicates the predicted times of high tide at the beach of collection. Broken lines indicate failure of the recording system (modified from Barnwell, 1966).

20

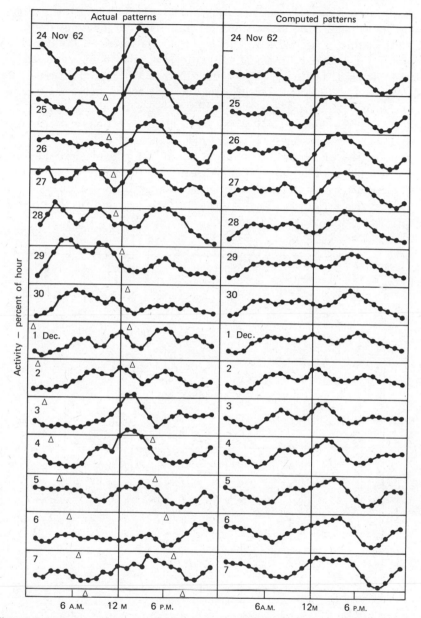

Figure 2-9. Comparison over a fortnight of the actual average daily patterns of activity of 10 fiddler crabs (*Uca mordax*) with the computed patterns for the same days. Triangles indicate the times of high tide at the site of collection (Belem, Brazil) (Barnwell, 1963).

Continuing their early studies on *U. pugnax,* Webb and Brown (1965) found that during the summers of 1961 and 1964, the phase of the daily rhythm in this organism had changed from the forenoon [as found by Bennett, Shriner, and Brown (1967)], the peak now being centered between 2300 and 0600 hours. They also discovered that the phase of the tidal rhythm in CC vacillated in a regular way as a function of time of the solar day (Figure 2-10). For example, between the hours of 2400 and 0500, the corresponding tidal peaks came about 3 h before the time of dead low tide; between 0800 and 1400 hours and between 1900 and 2400 hours this maximum was reached about 5–6 h before low tide; and between 1600 and 1900 hours it came quite close to the time of low tide. In their study it was the days during the change from one phase to the next that the period of the tidal rhythm was significantly lengthened or shortened, thus creating a "circatidal" frequency.

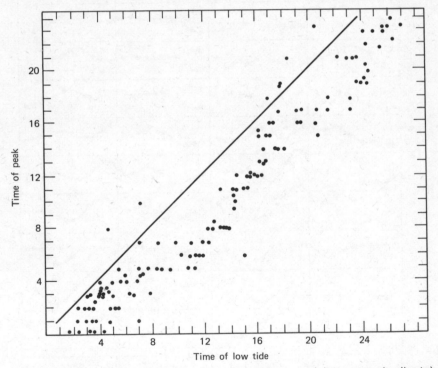

Figure 2-10. Time of day at which peak of locomotor activity occurs (ordinate) in relation to time of day of nearest low tide (abscissa). The diagonal line represents the coordinates that would be displayed if the activity peaks coincided with times of low tide. Each point is the average of 3–6 crabs (*Uca pugnax*) recorded in LL (<1 ft-c) (Webb and Brown, 1965).

This finding in LL is interesting in that the response is quite similar to the phase alterations of the natural tide. The intervals between tidal peaks vary in a rather regular way over the month, mainly as a result of solar gravitation. Between the spring and neap tides (Figure 1-8) the major role of the sun is to "prime" or "lag" the tidal crests—that is, to cause them to come earlier or later than they would normally (Nicholson, 1959). During these intervals the natural tides become circatidal. Returning to the crab again, the regular alterations of phase in their laboratory rhythms suggest that the pattern must be the combined expression of both the solar- and lunar-day clocks. When Webb and Brown repeated the experiment, now using LD, the rhythm was not circatidal (Figure 2-11).

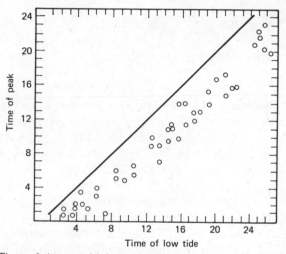

Figure 2-11. Time of day at which peak of locomotor activity occurs in relation to time of day of nearest low tide. The diagonal line represents the relationship that would be assumed if the activity peaks coincided with times of low tide. The crabs (*Uca pugnax*) were maintained in natural LD (modified from Webb and Brown, 1965).

Carcinus

The green crab, *Carcinus maenas* (Figure 2-12), has also been examined extensively for rhythmic behavior. In its littoral habitat it tends to reside under rocks or burrows during daytime low tides but ventures out underwater during daytime high tides and at night—safe times when it is not vulnerable to predation by herring gulls. Naylor (1958)

Figure 2-12. The green crab, *Carcinus maenas*.

studied its activity in CC in the lab in a saturated atmosphere or underwater. In either condition the activity was strongly rhythmic with peaks centered on the times of high tide (Figure 2-13). A solar-day component was also present in individual- and group-mean patterns, making itself manifest by augmenting nighttime tidal peaks (Figure 2-14). The rhythms lasted at least 6–7 days in CC. Blume, Bünning, and Müller (1962) and Powell (1962) have confirmed these findings.

Naylor (1960) next isolated his crabs from the tides in the laboratory but maintained them in natural LD cycles in an aquarium. At intervals he removed a few crabs for one-day sojourns in actographs in LL (dim). At first the test crabs displayed prominent tidal rhythms, but after 4 weeks this frequency had completely disappeared and the rhythmic behavior had become strictly nocturnal. Williams (1969) has reported that the tidal rhythm in the crab *Hemigrapsis edwardsi* also disappears after a time in the lab but then returns de novo.

Bliss and Sprague (1958) had shown that *Gecarcinus lateralis,* a land crab (as opposed to intertidal crabs such as *Uca* and *Carcinus*) had no tidal component in its persistent locomotor behavior. This was confirmed by Palmer (1971) and extended to three other species of land crabs. Naylor (1960, 1961) performed similar experiments on green crabs from essentially nontidal habitats: he collected *C. mediterraneus* from a Naples shoreline where the tidal exchange ranges over only 1.4 ft and *C. maenas* from a floating dock and placed them in CC. These crabs

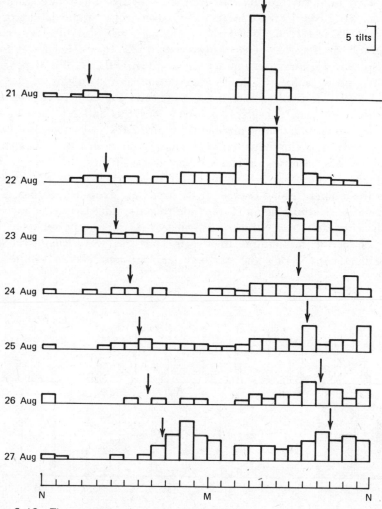

Figure 2-13. The average hourly activity of three green crabs (*Carcinus maenas*) over 7 days in LL (dim). The falling arrows signify the midpoints of high tides (Naylor, 1958).

displayed only circadian rhythms in the lab. However, the lack of a tidal rhythm in these crabs does not necessarily mean that they are devoid of this capacity. As will be described in detail in Chapter 8 (Figure 8-7), it was discovered that a *single* short cold pulse would induce a tidal frequency into the locomotor pattern of *C. maenas* taken from a non-tidal habitat (but was ineffective on *C. mediterraneus*) (Naylor, 1963).

In fact, tidal rhythmicity has been shown to be an innate feature of
C. maenas. Juvenile crabs were raised from eggs in the laboratory in
natural LD and 12°C. When they reached a size suitable for accurate
actograph studies, they were transferred to LL (dim). Each was found
to display a distinct circadian activity pattern with the initial peaks occurring during subjective nighttime. Periodogram analysis of the data
revealed that no tidal component was present (Figure 2-15A). The crabs
were then subjected to one 15-h interval of 4°C and returned to 15°C
and LL (dim). The tidal component (Figure 2-15B) was now also present
in the crabs with the first tidal peak coming on return to 15°C and subsequent peaks following at 12.4-h intervals (Williams and Naylor, 1967).
Since the chance that the crabs could have learned the 12.4-h period
from the ambient 24-h LD cycle or the one-time exposure to 15 h of low
temperature is slim, one must conclude that the tidal frequency is innate.

The tidal activity rhythm of *C. maenas* is apparently mediated by a
neuroendocrine mechanism in the eyestalk, as was demonstrated by
Powell (1965), Naylor and Williams (1968) and Naylor, Smith, and

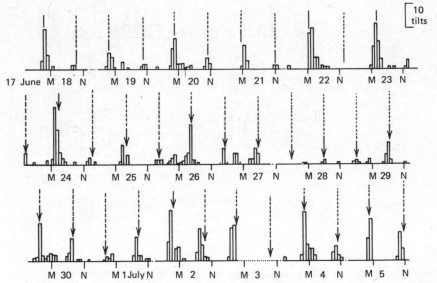

Figure 2-14. The daily activity pattern of 18 freshly collected green crabs
(*Carcinus maenas*) in LL (dim). Each day at 1400 hours a freshly collected
crab replaced the used one in the actograph. The design permitted the observer to see the amplitude enhancement of the nighttime tidal peak. The
falling arrows signify midpoints of high tides (Naylor, 1958).

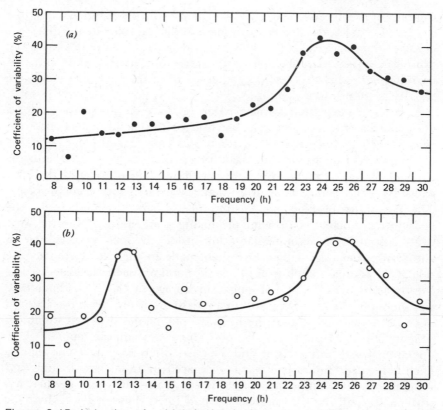

Figure 2-15. Induction of a tidal rhythm in the green crab (*Carcinus maenas*) by cold shock. Crabs were raised in the laboratory in natural LD cycles to a size suitable for actograph studies. In LL (dim) they displayed only a circadian rhythm as indicated by periodogram analysis (*a*). A subsequent single 15-h treatment at 4°C preceding return to LL (dim) initiated the tidal rhythm (*b*) (Williams and Naylor, 1967).

Williams (1973). Ablation of the stalk causes a temporary cessation of activity that gradually reestablishes itself to normal over a period of about 6 days. Because the green-crab tidal rhythm will persist only about 6 days in the laboratory, all crabs, eyestalkless or not, are arrhythmic by day 6. As mentioned previously, a 6-h exposure to 4°C will reinitiate the tidal rhythm in CC, so operated and control crabs now received this treatment: The eyestalkless crabs remained arrhythmic. In a follow-up experiment, only the retinae on the tips of the eyestalks were removed (thus blinding the crabs) and the animals were then subjected to a cold shock; the rhythm was reinstated, indicating that the X-organ/sinus-gland complex of the lower eyestalk must be the unit involved in mediating the rhythm. Eyestalk extracts were then made from crabs during the quiescent phase of their activity rhythm and injected into active eyestalkless crabs, causing a significant reduction in the level of activity. Apparently an inhibitor substance is periodically released from the stalk that molds the activity pattern into a rhythm.

A variety of experimental manipulations were employed to test for a hormonal basis to the locomotor rhythm of the penultimate-hour crab, *Sesarma reticulatum*. Eyestalk extracts made from crabs during either the peaks or troughs of their activity rhythm were injected into arrhythmic crabs, or 180° antiphase with the expressed cycles of rhythmic crabs. No effect was seen, showing that the eyestalks were not involved. The possibility of blood-borne substances liberated elsewhere in the body was eliminated as a rhythm-producing source in the following way: Crabs selected for accurate, large-amplitude rhythms were caused to autotomize their legs. Holes were then made in the exoskeleton to one side of the carapace midline of these crabs and of others that had become overtly arrhythmic because of long-term storage in CC. A rhythmic crab was then joined with sealing wax to an arrhythmic one, with the artificial opening juxtaposed so that the hemolymphs of the two were confluent (Figure 2-16). As drastic as the procedure may appear, only 3 of 50 operations were unsuccessful and survival often surpassed one month. Each homemade fusion pair was then placed in an actograph, and "its" spontaneous locomotion measured. Because the rhythmic partner was without legs, all recorded movements had to be those of the arrhythmic member. Any blood-borne locomotor promoting or inhibiting substances that might be produced rhythmically in the legless crab would be expected to be circulated to the peripatetic member, molding his response into a rhythm. In not one case was a rhythm recorded from such a parabiosed pair. On the other hand, a rhythm was always displayed when the conjunction was made between two rhythmic crabs, showing that the operation per se did not destroy expression of the rhythm (Palmer, unpublished).

Other Crustaceans

Buried in the sand high up on the beaches of southern California lives an amphipod, *Synchelidium sp*. At the peak of each high tide its habitat is covered with water and the tiny crustaceans emerge out of the fine sands to swim and feed in the wave wash. Two or three hours later the tide recedes and the amphipods reburrow to the comparative safety of their subterranean habitat. The persistence of this behavior, recorded as spon-

Figure 2-16. A parabiotic pair of penultimate-hour crabs (*Sesarma reticulatum*). Their hemolymphs are confluent via openings in their dorsal carapaces. The crab on top, which has cast off his legs (it is upside down; the bases of the legs are visible at the top of the picture), was selected for its precise, large-amplitude locomotor rhythm. The bottom crab was allowed to become arhythmic by long-term maintenance in CC. In no case was a blood-borne, rhythmically produced "locomotor" substance passed to the lower animal.

taneous activity in the constant conditions of the laboratory, has been studied by Enright (1963b).

Large populations of amphipods were placed in small seawater aquaria, where they spent their time either buried in the sandy bottom or swimming in the overlying water. The number swimming at any time was followed by time-lapse photography. A clear-cut persistent tidal rhythm was found that damped out after about three days. The first two peaks mimicked the phase, form, and semidiurnal inequality of the amplitude of the tides in the original habitat (Figure 2-17). After the first two peaks, the rhythm progressively deviated more from average tidal, the comparable daily peaks becoming considerably longer than 24.8 h.

Three other inhabitants of the same beach, an anomuran, *Emerita*; a mysid, *Archaeomysis*; and an isopod, *Excirolana*, all possessed a similar tidal rhythm, which became circatidal in the laboratory (Enright,

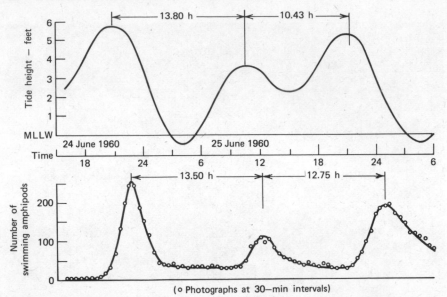

Figure 2-17. Tidal activity rhythm of the beach amphipod, *Synchelidium sp.,* in constant conditions. The upper graph represents predicted tides, and the lower graph, activity pattern of freshly collected amphipods during the same interval (modified from Enright, 1963b).

1963b). Almost identical rhythms have been reported in the amphipods *Corophium volutater* (Morgan, 1965), *Orchestia mediterranea* (Wildish, 1970), *Bathyporeia pelagica* (Fincham, 1970), *B. pelosa* (Preece, 1971), and *Marinogamarus marinus* (Fincham, 1972); the isopod *Eurydice pulchra* (Jones and Naylor, 1970; corroborated by Fish and Fish, 1972); and the prawns *Palaemon elegans* and *P. serratus* (Rodriguez and Naylor, 1972).

The isopod *Excirolana chiltoni* (Figure 2-18), a coinhabitant on *Synchelidium* beaches, also displays a persistent rhythm in which the amplitude and form mimic the waveform of the tides. On the shore it is subjected to tides that alternate between one and two crests per lunar day, which, furthermore, during the transitions from uni- to bimodal undergo a semidiurnal inequality in amplitude between peaks. Freshly collected animals reflect in the laboratory the form of the tides to which they were exposed just prior to collection. As seen in Figure 2-19A, isopods collected during a time when the tide consisted of only one peak per lunar day showed this frequency in CC. Animals subjected to two crests per lunar day, each of equal amplitude, expressed this to a great degree in the lab (Figure 2-19B). And finally, those taken during a bimodal stage

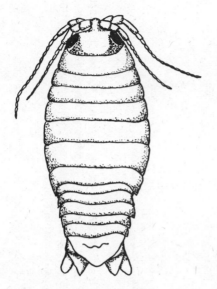

Figure 2-18. *Excirolana chiltoni* (modified from Klapow, 1972).

when the crests were of unequal amplitudes (Figure 2-19C), expressed this in the lab. In these studies there was usually no indication that the animals in CC mimicked the subsequent changes in waveform of the natural tide; for example, it is seen in Figure 2-19A that while the tides changed from one to two peaks per lunar day, the animals did not modify their rhythm accordingly. However, occasionally, the new tidal form was adopted spontaneously in CC (Figure 2-19B). The author (Klapow, 1972) states that the latter was not a consistent finding, but Enright (1972) (see below) found that it may be.

By improving his recording apparatus (Heusner and Enright, 1966), Enright (1972) was able to make long-term observations on individual isopods (*Excirolana chiltoni*). In his subsequent studies, he occasionally encountered an especially tenacious individual; one of them survived and continued to display its tidal rhythm for 65 days in CC. The period of this "virtuoso's" rhythm was circatidal, averaging 24 h and 55 min (Figure 2-20). The form of the rhythm mimicked the semidiurnal in-equality of the tides (as did *Synchelidium*), and the magnitude of the peaks was found to undergo a monthly rhythm: one peak decreased in amplitude, while the other increased and then vice versa—the process taking 30–31 days. Enright refers to this as a monthly rhythm in "ampli-tude modulation," which it is; and even more, it is a monthly rhythm in peak extinction, for during certain times of the month each peak is

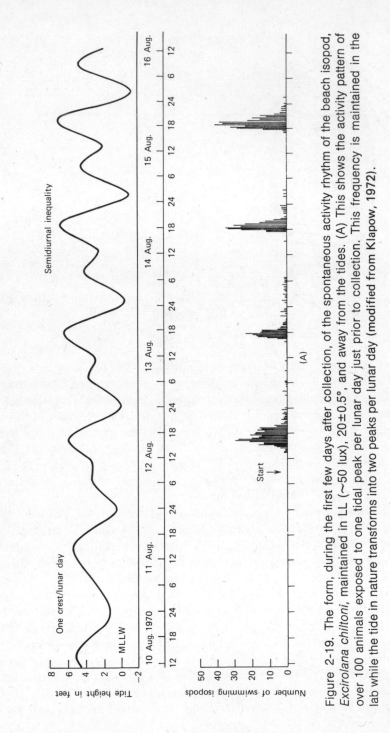

Figure 2-19. The form, during the first few days after collection, of the spontaneous activity rhythm of the beach isopod, *Excirolana chiltoni*, maintained in LL (~50 lux), 20±0.5°, and away from the tides. (A) This shows the activity pattern of over 100 animals exposed to one tidal peak per lunar day just prior to collection. This frequency is maintained in the lab while the tide in nature transforms into two peaks per lunar day (modified from Klapow, 1972).

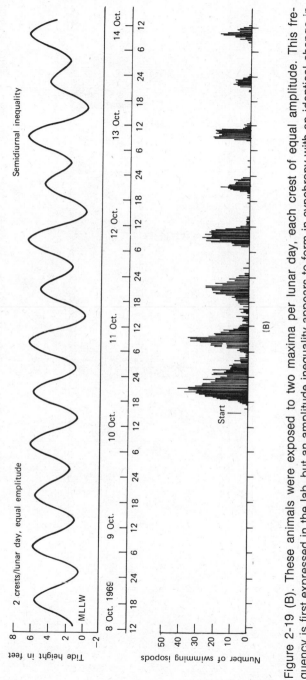

Figure 2-19 (B). These animals were exposed to two maxima per lunar day, each crest of equal amplitude. This frequency is first expressed in the lab, but an amplitude inequality appears to form in synchrony with an identical change in the natural tides. The author states that this was not a consistent finding in replicate studies (modified from Klapow, 1972).

33

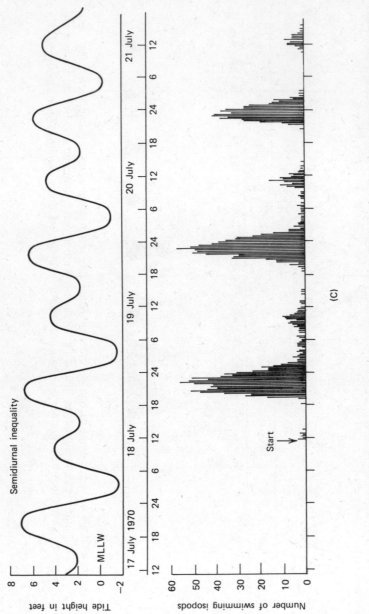

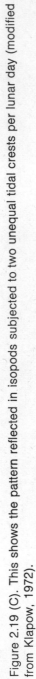

(C)

Figure 2.19 (C). This shows the pattern reflected in isopods subjected to two unequal tidal crests per lunar day (modified from Klapow, 1972).

34

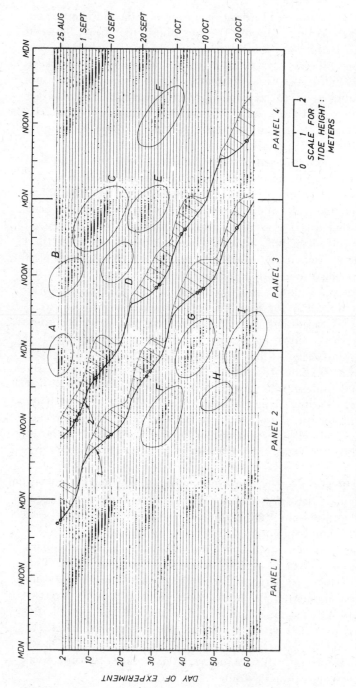

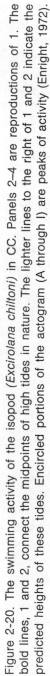

Figure 2-20. The swimming activity of the isopod (*Excirolana chiltoni*) in CC. Panels 2–4 are reproductions of 1. The bold lines, 1 and 2, connect the midpoints of high tides in nature. The lighter lines to the right of 1 and 2 indicate the predicted heights of these tides. Encircled portions of the actogram (A through I) are peaks of activity (Enright, 1972).

not only reduced in size, it is obliterated for several days. Enright concludes that the data do not "support the hypothesis that beats between the observed tidal rhythm and a hidden daily or circadian rhythm were responsible for the observed circa-lunar rhythm." He suggests a working hypothesis that includes "two tidal oscillators which are largely autonomous—although they tend to remain in 180° antiphase; and of 2 autonomous circa-lunar oscillators, each separately entrainable by the tidal regime, each associated with one of the tidal oscillators." Examining Figure 2-20, Panel 1, it is apparent that during the first 40 days in LL no tidal peaks were ever expressed between 2400 and 0900 hours and that as a peak approaches 2400 hours, it gradually diminishes in size, disappears between the "forbidden hours," and builds up after 0900 hours. This behavior, and then of course the whole monthly rhythm in peak extinction, could be explained by the interaction of a circadian rhythm (which, as previously described, is not uncommonly mixed with tidal rhythms) that has an increasing inhibitory action on the expression of the tidal peaks during these early morning hours. [Such an occultation mechanism has been postulated and developed in detail (Figure 3-5) by Palmer and Round (1967) for another shore-dwelling organism (it is discussed in Chapter 3).] Starting with day 42, the tidal peaks begin to encroach into the early morning hours, suggesting that the period of the circadian inhibitory rhythm has now begun to lengthen.

The anomuran crab, *Emerita asiatica*, is a filter feeder living in the intertidal zone and undergoes a rhythm similar to those just described. The crab digs itself backward into the sand and extends its featherlike antennae so as to filter the water that runs back to the ocean after each wave breaks. The crab allows itself to be washed shoreward with the flood tide and rides the waves seaward with ebb. Between waves it digs in and feeds.

In the lab in DD and a fairly constant temperature, this rhythm will persist for 3–4 days (Chandrashekaran, 1965). There is also the suggestion of a diurnal component that mandates that nighttime tidal peaks are always of greater amplitude.

The pink shrimp, *Penaeus duorarum*, lives buried in the sand during the day and, like most penaeid shrimp, emerges during the night. That light suppresses activity is part of shrimp-fisherman lore, as daytime catches are always augmented in murky water and in heavily overcast weather. When this crustacean is brought into the lab and placed in a seawater aquarium provided with a carpet of sand and offered LD 12:12, the nocturnal swimming pattern is especially prominent. In DD, the rhythm persists (Wickham, 1966; Hughes, 1968) and a second weak peak appears, suggesting a tidal rhythm.

During the life cycle of this animal a pelagic larva develops offshore and then moves or is displaced back to the intertidal zone. The post-larvae are easily netted on incoming tides. After their capture, either postlarvae or juvenile forms were placed in CC in a cylindrical tank equipped with a carrousel of paddles that created a clockwise current of constant intensity (Hughes, 1969); 2-min observations at 30-min inter-vals were made of the number of shrimp swimming, and their direction of motion (against or with the current) was recorded. It was found that postlarval shrimp swam against the current during the times correspond-ing to flood tide and with the current at the times of ebb in their old habitat. This tidal rhythm would persist for 3 days in the laboratory. On the other hand, only some of the juvenile shrimp displayed the same rhythm, and in them was apparent a daily component also, in that no downcurrent movements occurred during "daytime" low tides (Hughes, 1972).

Mollusks

The filter-feeding mussels, *Mytilus californianus* and *M. edulis,* often live in the intertidal zone, where they are periodically exposed to air. Rao (1954) has studied their filtration rates in CC by measuring the clearance rate of colloidal graphite from the surrounding water. He reports a tidal rhythm in this process that will persist for 4 wk (Figure 2-21A). Additional-ly, the water-propulsion tidal rhythm exists not only in intertidal in-habitants but also in members collected from the underside of a floating dock (where they are sheltered from the major viscissitudes of intertidal exchange) and from others living subtidally (in water 30 ft deep and there-fore not subjected to tidal exposure) (Figure 2-21B).

Another facet of mollusk feeding behavior is shell-gaping, the opening of the valves to permit extension of siphons or foot. In a summary review, Morton (1970) reports that tidal shell-gaping rhythms in bivalves under natural conditions are rather common. Gaping has been studied exten-sively in the laboratory in the quahog, *Merceneria (Venus) mercenaria,* and the oyster, *Crassostrea (Ostrea) virginica.* Early field observations by Loosanoff (1939) of the quahog indicated that shell-gaping was arrhyth-mic, and Bennett (1954) found this to be the case on a day-to-day basis. But when she combined 15-day units of continuous data, all collected in CC, she found statistical daily and tidal rhythmic trends. Palincsar (1958) confirmed this finding. Brown (1954) described similar rhythms in the oyster (Figure 6-1). The tidal component in both these animals expressed itself by causing augmented shell-gaping at the times of high tide. Enright (1965) has reanalyzed the above quahog and oyster data; and although

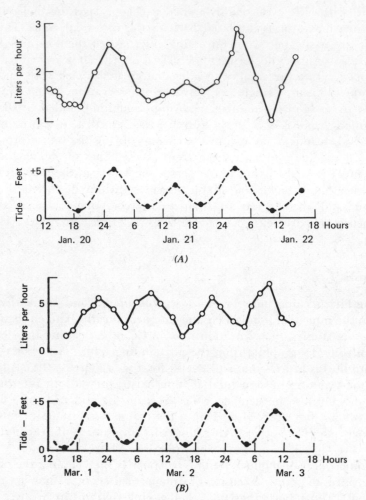

Figure 2-21. Rhythmic water propulsion in the mussel (*Mytilus californianus*) in DD and 14°C. (A) Mussel collected from the intertidal zone. (B) Mussel collected from the subtidal zone at a depth of 5 m (Rao, 1954).

he did not analyze for frequencies below 18 h, and specifically for a 12.4-h component (this reduces the sensitivity of the technique somewhat), he claims that spectral analysis does not disclose a tidal component in the data. His periodograms suggest that a circadian period is present in most sets of data.

A persistent locomotor activity rhythm in the snail, *Nassarius (Ilyanassa) obsoletus*, has been reported by Stephens, Sandeen, and Webb

(1953). Population averages of 10 snails revealed a tendency to be sluggish during the times of low tide and very active at high tides. The rhythm persisted for only 4 days in the lab but could be reestablished by a 24–48-h sojourn at 12°C (step-down from 22°C). More recent work has revealed the presence of overt circatidal activity rhythms in the gastropods *Bembicium nanum, Austrocochlea obtusa,* and the carnivorous welk, *Morula marginalba,* and both circatidal and circadian components in *Retina plicata* and *Melanerita atramentosa* (Zann, 1973).

VERTEBRATES

The shanny, *Blennius pholis,* a littoral fish living under loose stones in pools in the low-tide zone, feeds mainly on barnacles in the pools of the high-tide zone. As a consequence, it migrates between feeding and resting grounds with each flood tide.

Gibson (1965) studied the locomotor activity in this fish in the laboratory in an actograph designed to capitalize on the fact that the fish settles to the bottom of its container during inactive periods. Suspended from a counterbalanced lever and submerged in the aquarium was an elevatorlike platform; when the fish swam up off this platform, the latter would rise slightly and this motion was transcribed on a rotating kymograph drum (Figure 2-22). Recordings made in DD or LL, at a constant temperature and away from the tidal fluctuations, revealed that an overt near-tidal locomotor rhythm persisted for at least 4 days before

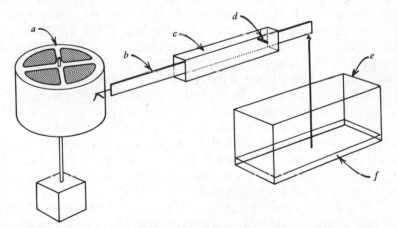

Figure 2-22. Elevator actograph apparatus used for recording locomotor activity in the shanny (*Blennus pholis*): *a,* kymograph; *b,* lever arm; *c,* limit box; *d,* fulcrum; *e,* aquarium; *f,* elevator platform (modified from Gibson, 1967).

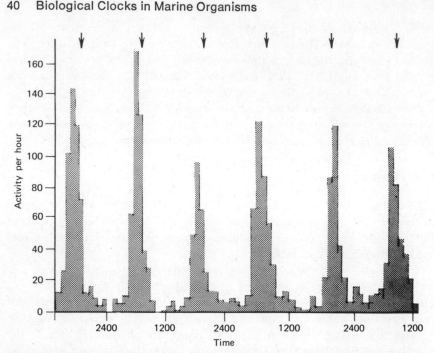

Figure 2-23. The persistent tidal activity rhythm of the shanny (*Blennius pholis*) in DD. Falling arrows show predicted time of high tide (modified from Gibson, 1965).

damping out (Figure 2-23). The period increased significantly from 12.4 to about 13 h in DD but not in LL. It is reported that there is not a daily rhythmic component in the pattern, but if the fish are kept in natural LD for 2–4 months, a daily rhythm eventually appears and will persist in DD (Gibson, 1965, 1967). Gibson (1970) has also reported a tidal activity rhythm in the intertidal fish *Coryphoblennius galerita.*

Just as Naylor (1961) had found with a Mediterranean species of green crab, Gibson (1969) found that *Blennius gattorugine* and *B. sanguino-lentus* from the same locale displayed only a circadian period in CC. The fish were collected from a Mediterranean coastline where the tidal exchange was a scant 18 cm. In LL (dim) or DD the fish expressed two peaks, one corresponding to the time of sunrise and the other sunset. This bimodal form is quite typical for circadian rhythms (Aschoff, 1966). Gibson speculated that it is conceivable that under strongly tidal conditions a biphasic rhythm such as this could be molded into one with peaks coinciding with the tides.

The Australian reef heron has been observed to fly from its inland rookery each day to the sea, so as to feed on the animals exposed during the times of low tides. Because the ebbing tide cannot be seen from the nesting area, it is suspected that the birds must possess a lunar-day clock that signals the feeding times 50 min later each day (Brown, 1958).

SUMMARY AND CONCLUSIONS

1. The activity patterns of 28 intertidal animals are discussed. All describe a periodicity with a basic component of 12.4 h, and this approximate period persists in the laboratory in constant light and temperature and in the absence of the tides. The duration of persistence ranges from a few cycles to months and is a function of the species studied, the conditions imposed, and individual tenacity.
2. In those few cases where relatively long-term observations have been made, the period of the rhythm tends to become obviously *circa*tidal.
3. In two separate studies, it was found that a natural LD cycle offered in the lab caused the persistent tidal rhythm to describe a strict 12.4-h period; in LL the period became *circa*tidal.
4. The "desired" phase relationship between rhythm and tidal cycle is species-specific. Geographic translocation experiments have shown that the phase is set by the local tides.
5. In some species the amplitude of the persistent rhythm mimics the diurnal inequality of the tides.
6. In about a third of the species discussed, a circadian component has been found combined with the tidal component. Many of the other studies were of such short duration that a low-amplitude circadian component would have gone unnoticed.
7. The tidal rhythm is innate. However, the rhythm sometimes (a) is lacking in organisms living in a nontidal habitat or (b) fades after a spell of incarceration in CC. Various treatments (which will be discussed in detail later)— some aperiodic—will induce the expression of the missing tidal rhythm.
8. In the green crab, removal of the eyestalks destroys the activity rhythm.

Literature Cited

Aschoff, J. 1965. Diurnal rhythms. *Ann. Rev. Physiol.*, 25:581–600.

Aschoff, J. 1966. Circadian activity patterns with two peaks. *Ecology*, 47:657–662.

Atkinson, R. J., and E. Naylor. 1973. Activity rhythms in some burrowing decapods. *Helgoländer wiss. Meeresunters*, 24:192–201.

Barnwell, F. H. 1963. Observations on daily and tidal rhythms in some fiddler crabs from equatorial Brazil. *Biol. Bull.*, 125:399–415.

Barnwell, F. H. 1966. Daily and tidal patterns of activity in individual fiddler crabs (Genus *Uca*) from the Woods Hole region. *Biol. Bull.*, 130:1–17.

Barnwell, F. H. 1968. The role of rhythmic systems in the adaptation of fiddler crabs to the intertidal zone. *Amer. Zool.*, 8:569–583.

Bennett, M. F. 1954. The rhythmic activity of the quahog, *Venus mercenaria*, and its modification by light. *Biol. Bull.*, 107:174–191.

Bennett, M. F., J. Shriner, and R. A. Brown. 1957. Persistent tidal cycles of spontaneous motor activity in the fiddler crab, *Uca pugnax*. *Biol. Bull.*, 112:267–275.

Bliss, D. E., and P. C. Sprague. 1958. Diurnal locomotor activity in *Gecarcinus lateralis*. *Anat. Rec.*, 132:416–417.

Blume, J., E. Bünning, and D. Müller. 1962. Periodenanalyse von Aktivitätsrhythmen bei *Carcinus maenas*. *Biol. Zbl.*, 81:569–573.

Brown, F. A., Jr. 1954. Persistent activity rhythms in the oyster. *Amer. J. Psysiol.*, 178:510–514.

Brown, F. A., Jr. 1958. The rhythmic nature of animals and plants. *Northwestern Tri-Quarterly*, Fall: 35–46.

Brown, F. A., Jr., M. F. Bennett, and H. M. Webb. 1954. Daily and tidal rhythms of O_2-consumption in fiddler crabs. *J. Cell. Comp. Physiol.*, 44:477–506.

Brown, F. A., Jr., R. O. Freeland, and C. L. Ralph. 1955. Persistent rhythms of O_2-consumption in potatoes, carrots and the seaweed, *Fucus*. *Plant Physiol.*, 30:280–292.

Brown, F. A., Jr., and H. M. Webb. 1948. Temperature relations of an endogenous daily rhythmicity in the fiddler crab, *Uca*. *Physiol. Zool.*, 21:371–381.

Brown, F. A., Jr., R. A. Brown, H. M. Webb, M. Bennett, and J. Shriner. 1956. A persistent tidal rhythm of locomotor activity in *Uca pugnax*. *Anat. Rec.*, 125:613–614.

Chandrashekaran, M. K. 1965. Persistent tidal and diurnal rhythm of locomotor activity and oxygen consumption in *Emerita asiatica* (M.Edw) *Z. vergl. Physiol.*, 50:137–150.

Chapman, S., and J. Bartels. 1940. *Geomagnetism*. Clarendon, Oxford.

Dembowski, J. B. 1926. Notes on the behavior of the fiddler crab. *Biol. Bull.*, 50:179–201.

Enright, J. T. 1963a. Endogenous tidal and lunar rhythms. *Proc. XVI Inter. Cong. Zool.*, 4:355–359.

Enright, J. T. 1963b. The tidal rhythm of activity of an sand-beach amphipod. *Z. vergl. Physiol.*, 46:276–313.

Enright, J. T. 1965. The search for rhythmicity in biological time-series. *J. Theoret. Biol.*, 8:426–468.

Enright, J. T. 1972. A virtuoso isopod. Circa-lunar rhythms and their tidal fine structure. *J. Comp. Physiol.*, 77:141–162.

Fincham, A. A. 1970. Rhythmic behaviour of the intertidal amphipod *Bathyporeia pelagica. J. mar. biol. Ass. U.K.,* 50:1057–1068.

Fincham, A. A. 1972. Rhythmic swimming and rheotropism in the amphipod *Marinogamarus marinus. J. exp. mar. Biol. Ecol.* 8:19–26.

Fish, J. D., and S. Fish. 1972. The swimming rhythm of *Eurydice pulchra* and a possible explanation of intertidal migration. *J. exp. mar. Biol. Ecol.,* 8:195–200.

Gibson, R. N. 1965. Rhythmic activity in littoral fish. *Nature,* 207:544–545.

Gibson, R. N. 1967. Experiments on the tidal rhythm of *Blennius pholis. J. mar. biol. Ass. U.K.,* 47:97–111.

Gibson, R. N. 1969. Activity rhythm in two species of *Blennius* from the Mediterranean. *Vie et Milieu, Ser. A,* 20:235–244.

Gibson, R. N. 1970. The tidal rhythm of activity of *Coryphoblennius galerita. Anim. Behav.,* 18:539–543.

Herrnkind, W. F. 1968. Adaptive visually-directed orientation in *Uca pugilator. Amer. Zool.,* 8:585–598.

Heusner, A. A., and J. T. Enright. 1966. Long-term activity recording in small aquatic animals. *Science,* 154:532–533.

Honegger, H.-W. 1973. Rhythmic motor activity responses of the California fiddler crab *Uca crenulata* to artificial light conditions. *Mar. Biol.,* 18:19–31.

Hughes, D. A. 1968. Factors controlling emergence of pink shrimp (*Penaeus duorarum*) from the substrate. *Biol. Bull.,* 134:48–59.

Hughes, D. A. 1972. On the endogenous control of tide-associated displacements of pink shimp, *Penaeus duorarum. Biol. Bull.,* 142:271–280.

Hyman, O. W. 1920. Adventures in the life of a fiddler crab. *Ann. Rept. Smithson. Inst.,* pp. 443–459.

Jones, D. A., and E. Naylor. 1970. The swimming rhythm of the sand beach isopod *Eurydice pulchra. J. exp. mar. Biol. Ecol.,* 4:188–199.

Klapow, L. A. 1972. Natural and artificial rephasing of a tidal rhythm. *J. Comp. Physiol.,* 79:233–258.

Loosanoff, V. L. 1939. Effect of temperature upon shell movements of clams, *Venus mercenaria. Biol. Bull.,* 76:171–182.

Morgan, E. 1965. The activity rhythm of the amphipod *Corophium volutator* (Pallas) and its possible relationship to changes in hydrostatic pressure associated with the tides. *J. Anim. Ecol.,* 34:731–746.

Morton, B. 1970. The tidal rhythm and rhythm of feeding and digestion in *Cardium edule. J. mar. biol. Ass. U.K.,* 50:488–512.

Naylor, E. 1958. Tidal and diurnal rhythms of locomotory activity in *Carcinus maenas* (L). *J. Exp. Biol.,* 35:602–610.

Naylor, E. 1960. Locomotory rhythms in *Carcinus maenas* (L) from non-tidal conditions. *J. Exp. Biol.*, 37:482–488.

Naylor, E. 1961. Spontaneous locomotor rhythm in mediterranean *Carcinus. Pubbl. Staz. Zool. Napoli*, 32:58–63.

Naylor, E. 1963. Temperature relationships of the locomotor rhythm of *Carcinus. J. Exp. Biol.*, 40:669–679.

Naylor, E., G. Smith, and B. G. Williams. 1973. The role of the eyestalk in the tidal activity rhythm of the shore crab *Carcinus maenas* (L). In: Neurobiology of Invertebrates, Hungarian Academy of Sciences, pp. 423–429.

Naylor, E., and B. G. Williams. 1968. Effects of eyestalk removal on rhythmic locomotor activity in *Carcinus. J. Exp. Biol.*, 49:107–116.

Nicholson, T. D. 1959. The tides. *Nat. Hist.*, 68:327–333.

Palincsar, J. 1958. Periodisms in amount of spontaneous activity in the quahog, *Venus mercenaria*. Doctoral diss., Northwestern University.

Palmer, J. D. 1963. "Circa-tidal" activity rhythms in fiddler crabs. Effect of light intensity. *Biol. Bull.*, 125:387.

Palmer, J. D. 1964. A persistent, light-preference rhythm in the fiddler crab, *Uca pugnax*, and its possible adaptive significance. *Amer. Nat.*, 98:431–434.

Palmer, J. D. 1967. Daily and tidal components in the persistent rhythmic activity of the crab, *Sesarma. Nature*, 215:64–66.

Palmer, J. D. 1971. Comparative studies of circadian locomotory rhythms in four species of terrestrial crabs. *Am. Midl. Nat.*, 85:97–107.

Palmer, J. D. 1973. Tidal rhythms: the clock control of the rhythmic physiology of marine organisms. *Biol. Rev.*, 48:377–418.

Pearse, A. S. 1914. On the habitats of *U. pugnax* and *U. pugilator. Trans. Wis. Acad. Sci. Arts Lett.*, 17:791–805.

Powell, B. L. 1962. Studies on rhythmical behaviour in crustacea. I. Persistent locomotor activity in juvenile *Carcinus maenas* (L) and in *Ligia oceanica* (L). *Crustaceana*, 4:42–46.

Powell, B. L. 1965. The hormonal control of the tidal rhythm of locomotory activity in *Carcinus maenas. Gen. Comp. Endocrin.*, 5: Abst. 84.

Preece, G. S. 1971. The swimming rhythm of *Bathyporeia pilosa. J. mar. biol. Ass. U.K.*, 51:777–791.

Rao, K. P. 1954. Tidal rhythmicity of rate of water propulsion in *Mytilus*, and its modifiability by transplantation. *Biol. Bull.*, 106: 353–359.

Rodriguez, G., and E. Naylor. 1972. Behavioural rhythms in littoral prawns. *J. mar. biol. Ass. U.K.*, 52:81–95.

Schwartz, B., and S. R. Safir. 1915. The natural history and behavior of the fiddler crab. *Cold Spring Harbor Monogr.*, 8:1–24.

Stephens, G. C., M. I. Sandeen, and H. M. Webb. 1953. A persistent tidal rhythm of activity in the mud snail, *Nassa obsoleta. Anat. Rec.*, 117:635.

Webb, H. M., and F. A. Brown, Jr. 1965. Interactions of diurnal and tidal rhythms in the fiddler crab, *Uca pugnax. Biol. Bull.*, 129:582–591.

Wickham, D. A. 1966. Observations on the patterns of persistent activity in juvenile pink shrimp, *Penaeus duorarum.* M.S. thesis, University of Miami.

Wildish, F. J. 1970. Locomotor activity rhythms in some littoral *Orchestia. J. mar. biol. Ass. U.K.,* 50:241–252.

Williams, B. G. 1969. The rhythmic activity of *Hemigrapsus edwardsi. J. exp. mar. Biol. Ecol.,* 3:215–223.

Williams, B. G., and E. Naylor. 1967. Spontaneously induced rhythm of tidal periodicity in laboratory-reared *Carcinus. J. Exp. Biol.,* 47:229–234.

Zann, L. P. 1973. Relationships between intertidal zonation and circatidal rhythmicity in littoral gastropods. *Mar. Biol.,* 18:243–250.

3 Vertical Migration Rhythms

In the sands of certain beaches in Brittany, in a narrow zone just below the high-water mark of neap tides, lives a small acoelous turbellarian, *Convoluta roscoffensis* (Figure 3-1). At night and during high tides this zooanthellae-bearing worm lives in the interstices between sand grains but emerges onto the sediment surface during daytime low tides. Exposure to direct sunlight allows photosynthetic reserves to build up in the symbiotic alga, some of which is subsequently used by the planarians. In spite of the fact that the adult worm reaches a length of only 4 mm, it is present in such enormous numbers (28×10^6 worms/m²) that large expanses of beach sand appear spinach green during daytime low tides. Just before the flooding tide covers these patches, the gregarious worms rapidly burrow beneath the sand and thus avoid the risk of being washed away. With the advent of the next daytime low tide the worms again emerge onto the surface (Gamble and Keeble, 1903; Keeble, 1910). These commutations are referred to as *vertical migrations*.

If sand samples bearing these animals are brought into the laboratory and placed in constant light and away from the tides, the vertical migrations continue for 4–7 days in approximate synchrony with the tides (Bohn, 1903; Martin, 1907). That a phototactic response is involved in the rhythm is indicated by the fact that the rhythm will persist in constant light but not in constant darkness.

Diatoms (Fauvel and Bohn, 1907; Aleem, 1949; Callame and Debyser, 1954) and euglenoids (Bracher, 1919, 1937) are also known to undergo vertical-migration rhythms on the tidal shore; these rhythms are reported to persist in natural LD cycles in the lab for a few days. However, only Palmer and Round (1965), Palmer (1967b), and Round and Palmer (1966) have studied any of these species in CC for protracted periods of time. Following the migrations of two species of *Euglena* and eight species of diatoms in the constancy of the laboratory, they found, surprisingly, that the rhythm was not tidal, but daily (Figure 3-2). When figures in past publications were then reexamined, it was found that

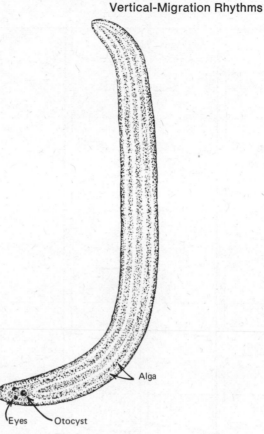

Figure 3-1. *Convoluta roscoffensis* (Keeble, 1910).

the curves, which spanned only 1–3 days, were not at all convincingly tidal. The previous interpretation that they represented tidal rhythms could well have been predicated on the fact that that was the expected response. In view of this new finding, a hypothesis was constructed stating that in the natural habitat the basic daily rhythm was transformed into a tidal pattern by the periodic darkening created by the very turbid flood tides. This hypothesis gained strength from the work of Perkins (1960), who found that the diatoms he studied in the extremely transparent water of the River Eden in Scotland appeared on the surface throughout each span of daylight regardless of the state of the tide.

Alone among the modern studies in contradiction to our new hypothesis is the work of Fauré-Fremiet (1951) on the diatom *Hantzschia amphioxys* (later reidentified as *H. virgata*) and possibly also his study on the chrysomonad, *Chromulina* (1950). He exposed *Hantzschia*-bearing

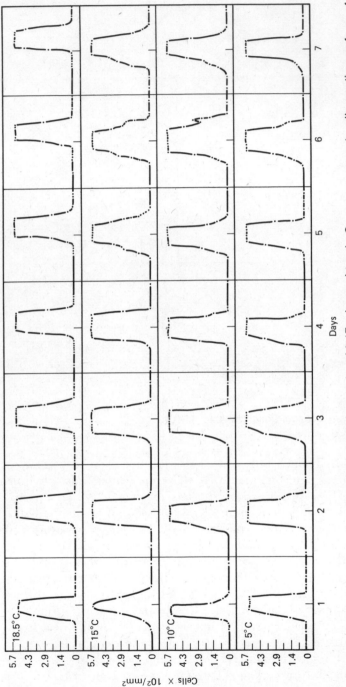

Figure 3-2. The vertical-migration rhythm of the euglenoid (*Euglena obtusa*). Curves represent cells on the surface of mud samples. In their natural habitat on the banks of the River Avon, the euglena burrow up out of the mud only during daytime low tides. In the laboratory in LL (98 ft-c) and the contant temperatures indicated, other than the first day in captivity, only broad peaks representing a diurnal rhythm are displayed. Note that at 18.5°C the period of the rhythm is lengthened to 24.5 h ($Q_{10} = \sim 0.94$) (Palmer and Round, 1965).

sand samples on a windowsill and on 6 consecutive days found that the diatoms "reappeared on the surface of the sand at the same time as low tide in their natural habitat." Palmer and Round (1967) have reexamined this organism's rhythm and confirmed his findings, learning additionally that the tidal period would also persist in LL (Figure 3-3) for at least 11 days. The rhythm is intimately involved with a rhythm in phototaxis (Palmer, 1960). The adaptive significance of the movements are supposedly to expose the sand-dwelling diatoms to bright sunlight so that they may undergo maximum photosynthesis and to reburrow in time so as not to be washed away (Ganapti, Rao, and Rao, 1959). However, Taylor and Palmer (1963) have found that *Hantzschia* is a "shade species" and that sufficient light penetrates the sand to obviate the need of a trip to the surface for photosynthesis.

The *Hantzschia* rhythm differs from most other tidal rhythms in that only one peak per lunar day is expressed and it appears only between sunrise and sunset. When expressed, the peak proceeds across the solar day at a proper tidal progression rate of 50 min/day. When the peak reaches sunset, it dissolves over a few days, while a morning peak is reconstituted simultaneously (Figure 3-4).

That the onset of darkness is not the stimulus for a rapid rephase backward to sunrise (or "light-on" in the laboratory) was demonstrated by keeping the diatoms in LL: the rephase occurred as usual (Figure 3-4). In fact, this unique behavior is not even interpreted as a rephase but instead as the overt display of a normal, two-peaks-per-day tidal rhythm interacting with a daily rhythm. As described diagrammatically in Figure 3-5, the daily rhythm consists of alternating portions that override the tidal rhythms and permit or repress the expression of either of the tidal peaks. The repression phase of the 24-h rhythm occurs during the hours corresponding to nighttime. When the late-afternoon tidal peak begins to straddle the repression peak of the daily rhythm, it is damped to extinction over an interval of about 3 days. Simultaneously, the other tidal peak moves (at a rate of 50 min/day) out from under the repressive influence of the daily rhythm and is expressed in the early morning hours.

Vertical-migration rhythms are also known for deep-water organisms. In fact, as early as 1817 (Curvier) it was known that some zooplankton migrated through a vertical distance of several hundred meters from the depths during daytime to the surface waters at night. So well documented was the role of light and dark in the control of these movements (see, for example, Harris and Wolfe, 1955; Backus, Clark, and Wing,

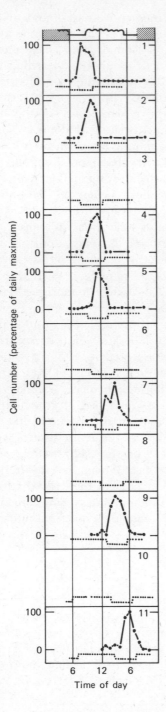

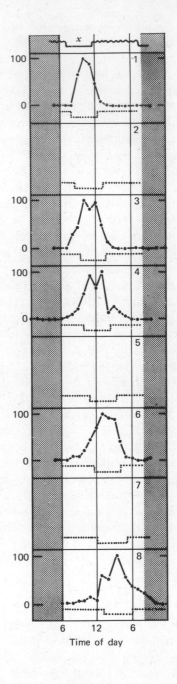

Cell number (percentage of daily maximum)

Time of day

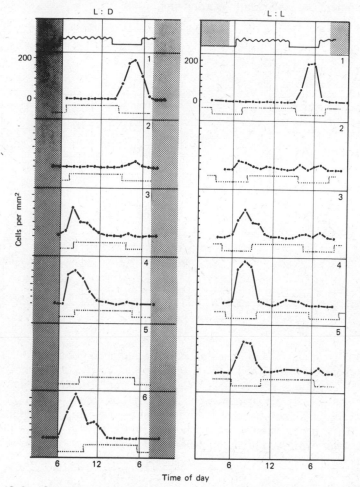

Time of day

Figure 3-3. (*Opposite page*) The persistent vertical-migration rhythm in the pennate diatom, *Hantzschia virgata,* in LL (110 ft-c) (left-hand column) and LD 14.5:9.5 (110 ft-c) (right-hand column). Curves represent the number of cells (expressed in percentages) on the surfaces of sand samples (in no case was 100% represented by less than 2.9×10^3 cells/cm²). Consecutive days are represented one beneath the other; stippling indicates the hours of darkness; x is time of collection of sample in the field; and intervals of low tide in the natural habitat are symbolized by depressed segments of dotted lines subtending the curves (Palmer and Round, 1967).

Figure 3-4. (*This page*) The clock programmed phase change in the vertical-migration of the diatom *Hantzschia virgata* in LD 14.5:9.5 (110 ft-c) and LL (110 ft-c). Symbols the same as in Figure 3-3 (Palmer and Round, 1967).

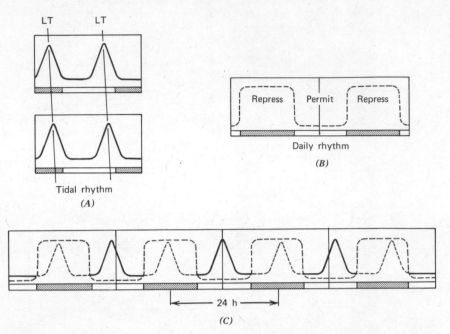

Figure 3-5. Diagrammatic representation of the interaction of a 24.8-h bimodal vertical migration rhythm and a 24-h suppression–expression rhythm. (A) A typical tidal rhythm with two peaks per day, coming 50 min later each day. (B) A typical solar-day rhythm, this one having a postulated function of either permitting or inhibiting—depending on its phase—the expression of the tidal rhythm. (C) The combined action of the two, the solid line representing the overt behavior expressed to the observer (LT=midpoints of low tides; shaded bars=hours of darkness).

1965) that there was no reason to suspect that the rhythms might persist in constant conditions.

However, ecological observations had shown that many of these rhythms were also characterized by a midnight sinking followed by a second rise to the surface at dawn, an occurrence not predicted by changes in illumination. Also, a crustacean whose cyclopean eye had been surgically removed still carried out the typical sequence of vertical migrations (Harris and Mason, 1956), certainly suggesting that control of the rhythm was more complicated than originally expected.

In fact, as early as 1917 (Esterley), experimental evidence had been obtained that suggested that vertical migration rhythms would persist in constant conditions. In the laboratory in DD two species of copepods (*Acartia* and *Calanus*) were found more frequently at the top of a water column between 1800 and 2000 hours than any other time of day. Follow-up experiments did not confirm these results. Then, in 1963, Harris demonstrated convincingly that the rhythm was clock-controlled in a laboratory population of *Daphnia magna* and *Calanus finmarchicus*. In a glass tank in LL or DD, he determined photographically (in red light) the hourly position of these plankton populations within the container. As can be seen in Figure 3-6, the vertical-migration rhythm per-

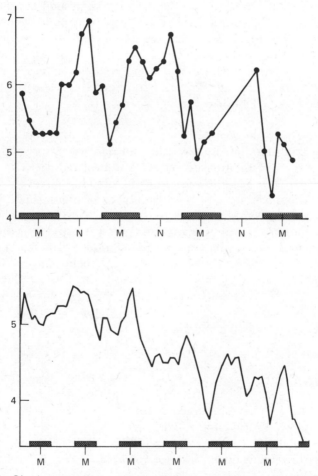

Figure 3-6. Clock-controlled vertical-migration rhythm in *Daphnia magna* in DD (top curve) and LL (dim) (lower curve). Ordinate values are arbitrary units each equal to one-tenth the depth of the water in the tank. Shaded bars on abscissa represent nighttime outside the laboratory (M=midnight). The period of the rhythms in DD=24 h; in LL. 28 h (modified from Harris, 1963).

sisted in both constant darkness or constant light. As expected, the length of the period depended on the intensity of the constant illumination: it was 24 h in darkness and 28 h in light.

Enright and Hamner (1967) studied the vertical-migration rhythm of a natural plankton population maintained in a large concrete tank 2.5 m deep, over which the lighting could be controlled. They dipped the plankton from the surface waters of the tank with hand nets at 3-h intervals in normal light–dark cycles and in LL (dim). Of the many species present, the amphipod *Nototropis*; the isopod *Exosphaeroma*; the cumacean *Cyclopis*; and the teltidiad copepods underwent *persistent* vertical-migration rhythms. Other organisms present migrated in the light–dark conditions also but not in constant dim illumination. While no distinct persistent rhythm was found in *Acartia*, peaks of relative abundance were noted at the times corresponding to twilight, just as Esterley had reported 50 years earlier.

A rather amusing and puzzling phenomenon was discovered after the atomic explosion at Bikini—a diurnal rhythm of radioactivity in *battleships!* Strangely, the radiation level of the surviving target ships, instead of steadily diminishing, rose measurably each night. Field ecologists were soon able to show that the rhythm was a direct correlate of the diurnal migration rhythm of plankton. After the explosion, these microorganisms "swallowed" great quantities of radioactive material. Their nightly excursions to the ocean surface placed them in vulnerable proximity to the grasping cirri of the barnacles attached to the ship bottoms, and as the barnacles captured more of these organisms at night, their radiation level increased sufficiently to affect the value of a given ship as a whole (Fraser, 1962).

Literature Cited

Aleem, A. 1949. The diatom community inhabiting the mud-flats at Whitestable. *New Phytol.*, 49:274–287.

Backus, R. H., R. C. Clark, and A. S. Wing. 1965. Behaviour of certain marine organisms during the solar eclipse of July 21, 1963. *Nature*, 205:989–991.

Bohn, G. 1903. Sur les movements oscillatoires des *Convoluta roscoffensis*. *C.R. Acad. Sci.* (Paris), 137:576–578.

Bracher, R. 1919. Observations on *Euglena deses*. *Ann. Bot.*, 33:93–108.

Bracher, R. 1937. The light relations of *Euglena limosa* Gard. Part I.

The influence of intensity and quality of light on phototaxy. *J. Linn. Soc. (Bot.)*, 51:23–42.

Callame, B., and J. Debyser. 1954. Observations sur les mouvements des diatomées a la surface des sédiments marins de la zone intercotidale. *Vie et Milieu*, 5:242–249.

Cuvier, Le Baron. 1817. *Le Régne animal*. Paris.

Enright, J. T., and W. M. Hamner. 1967. Vertical diurnal migration and endogenous rhythmicity. *Science,* 157:937–941.

Esterly, C. O. 1917. The occurrence of a rhythm in the geotropism of two species of plankton copepods when certain recurring external conditions are absent. *Univ. Calif. Publ. Zool.*, 16:393–400.

Fauré-Fremiet, E. 1950. Rythme de maree d'un *Chromulina psammophile*. *Biol. Bull.*, 84:207–214.

Fauré-Fremiet, E. 1951. The tidal rhythm of the diatom *Hantzchia amphioxys*. *Biol. Bull.*, 100:173–177.

Fauvel, P., and G. Bohn. 1907. Le rhythme des marees chez les diatommees littorales. *C.R. Soc. Biol.* (Paris), 62:121–123.

Fraser, J. 1962. *Nature Adrift*. Foulis, London.

Gamble, F. W., and F. Keeble. 1903. The bionomics of *Convoluta roscoffensis*, with special reference to its green cells. *Proc. Royal Soc.* (London), 72:93–98.

Ganapti, P. N., M. V. L. Rao, and D. U. S. Rao. 1959. Tidal rhythms of some diatoms and dinoflagellates inhabiting the intertidal sands of the Visakhapatnam beach. *Current Sci.* (India), 28:450–451.

Harris, J. E. 1963. The role of endogenous rhythms in vertical migration. *J. mar. biol. Ass. U.K.*, 43:153–166.

Harris, J. E., and P. Mason. 1956 Vertical migration in eyeless *Daphnia*. *Proc. Roy. Soc.* (London), Ser. B, 145:280–290.

Harris, J. E., and U. K. Wolfe. 1955. A laboratory study of vertical migration. *Proc. Roy. Soc.* (London), Ser. B, 144:329–354.

Keeble, F. 1910. *Plant Animals*. Cambridge University Press, Cambridge.

Martin, L. 1907. La mémoire chez *Convoluta roscoffensis*. *C.R. Acad. Sci.* (Paris), 145:555–557.

Palmer, J. D. 1960. The role of moisture and illumination on the expression of the rhythmic behavior of the diatom, *Hantzschia amphioxys*. *Biol. Bull.*, 119:330.

Palmer, J. D. 1967. *Euglena* and the tides. *Nat. Hist.*, 76:60 64.

Palmer, J. D., and F. E. Round. 1965. Persistent, vertical-migration rhythms in benthic microflora. I. The effect of light and temperature on the rhythmic behaviour of *Euglena obtusa*. *J. mar. biol. Ass. U.K.*, 45:567–582.

Palmer, J. D., and F. E. Round. 1967. Persistent, vertical-migration

rhythms in benthic microflora. VI. The tidal and diurnal nature of
the rhythm in the diatom *Hantzschia virgata*. *Biol. Bull.*, 132:44–55.

Perkins, E. J. 1960. The diurnal rhythm of the littoral diatoms of the
River Eden estuary, Fife. *J. Ecol.*, 48:725–728.

Round, F. E., and J. D. Palmer. 1966. Persistent, vertical-migration
rhythms in benthic microflora. II. Field and laboratory studies of
diatoms from the banks of the River Avon. *J. mar. biol. Assn. U.K.*,
46:191–214.

Taylor, W. R., and J. D. Palmer. 1963. The relationship between light
and photosynthesis in intertidal benthic diatoms. *Biol. Bull.*, 125:395.

4 Color-Change Rhythms

FIDDLER CRABS

In the hypodermis of the fiddler crab, *Uca,* are located black, red white, and yellow chromatophores. These stellate cells contain their pigment granules distributed between two extreme phases: concentrated into a single spot in the cell center or evenly dispersed throughout the cytoplasm. In the latter phase the animal takes on the general color of the chromatophores. In 1912, Megušar noted that *U. pugnax* in the field underwent a daily color change, being dark during the daytime and pale at night.

To quantify the degree of color change for accurate study of the rhythm in the laboratory, pigment dispersion within the chromatophores was divided arbitrarily into five stages (Hogben and Slome, 1931), as in Figure 4-1. The changes are most easily observed, and therefore pigment dispersion most quickly staged, on the meropod segments of the legs.

Abramowitz (1937) showed that this rhythm would persist in *U. pugnax* and *U. pugilator* in either DD or dim LL, the former being more favorable for the extended expression of the rhythm. Brown and Webb (1948) (Figure 4-2) confirmed Abramowitz's discovery, and Brown (1950) extended this to the red chromatophores of *U. pugilator.* Using the average response of large sample populations, the above authors (Brown and Webb) reported that the period of the persistent rhythm was exactly 24 h. However, Stephens (1962) followed the rhythms of individual crabs and found that some had periods either longer or shorter than 24 h, and a few were as much as 180° out of phase with the rhythm displayed in nature. But, when he lumped his results together, the maxi periods canceled out the mini ones and the population average was indistinguishable from 24 h.

All through the course of the above studies the observers found day-to-day differences in the form and amplitude of the rhythm that appeared to be beyond the range of observational error. A comprehensive study

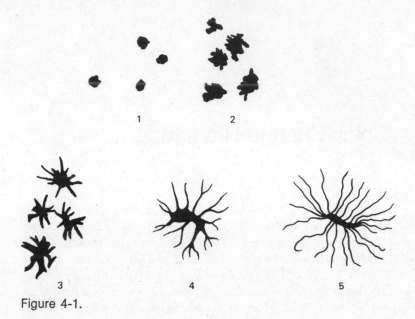

Figure 4-1.

was thus undertaken using large numbers of animals, and it was found that the daily rhythm of melanin dispersion was supplemented by a tidal rhythmic component that persisted for 2–3 weeks in CC (Brown, Fingerman, Sandeen, and Webb, 1953). Because the chromatophore pigments remained concentrated at night, the tidal component made itself manifest only during the day by causing increased melanin dispersion around the times of low tide (Figure 4-3). The presence of this component in *U. pugnax* was corroborated by Hines (1954): and Fingerman (1956) got similar results with *U. pugilator* and *U. speciosa*. Although a pigment-dispersion hormone is known to be produced in the eyestalk, it was demonstrated (Webb, Bennett, and Brown, 1954) and confirmed 10 years later (Fingerman and Yamamoto, 1964) that the color-change rhythm would persist, but with much reduced amplitude, in eyestalkless crabs in CC.

Barnwell (1963) has studied color change in three Brazilian fiddler crabs, *U. mordax, U. rapax,* and *U. maracoani*. In LL (dim), all three species displayed daily melanophore activity rhythms, which had average free running periods of about 25 h in populations of *U. mordax* and *U. rapax*. No mention is made of a tidal component in the data, but he reports that two of the three species display tidal running rhythms. Nor was this component reported in the daily color change rhythm of *Sesarma* (Fingerman, Nagabhushanam, and Philpott, 1961), a crab also known

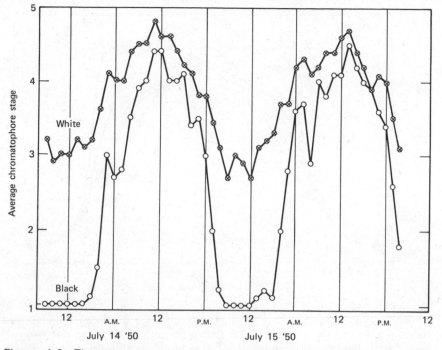

Figure 4-2. The average color change patterns of 50 fiddler crabs (*Uca pugnax*) over 48 h in DD. The curves signify the degree of pigment dispersion in the white and black chromatophores (modified from Brown, Fingerman, Sandeen, and Webb, 1953).

to have a prominent tidal component in its locomotor activity (Palmer, 1967).

Fingerman (1956) and Fingerman, Lowe, and Mobberly (1958) studied *U. pugilator* and *U. speciosa* from the Gulf of Mexico, collected from a habitat subjected to only one high tide each lunar day. In DD they found that the tidal component of the color-change rhythm did not display the expected 24.8 h unimodal period, but was instead a bimodal lunar day rhythm. Fingerman (1955) has published an identical finding for the blue crab, *Callinectes sapidus*.

GREEN CRABS

Powell (1962a,b; 1966) has described a circadian color-change rhythm in juvenile green crabs (*Carcinus maenas*). He found no tidal component in the data. Also, unlike *Uca*, the rhythm did not persist in the absence of the eyestalks, but when eyestalks from rhythmic animals were implanted, the rhythm reappeared.

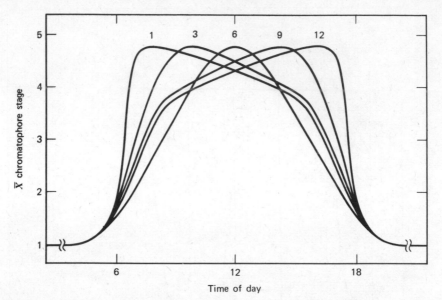

Figure 4-3. Digrammatic representation of the amplitude modulating effect of a tidal rhythmic component on a daily (color-change) rhythm. The composite shows the sequential changes in the amplitude and form of the daily rhythm during a 12-day interval. Curve 1 represents the form of the rhythm on day 1; curve 12, twelve days later.

Literature Cited

Abramowitz, A. 1937. The chromatophorotropic hormones of the crustacea: standardization, properties and physiology of the eye-stalk glands. *Biol. Bull.,* 72:344–365.

Barnwell, F. H. 1963 Observations on daily and tidal rhythms in some fiddler crabs from equatorial Brazil. *Biol. Bull.,* 125:399–415.

Brown, F. A., Jr. 1950. Studies on the physiology of *Uca* red chromatophores. *Biol. Bull.,* 98:218–226.

Brown, F. A., Jr., M. Fingerman, M. Sandeen, and H. M. Webb. 1953. Persistent diurnal and tidal rhythms of color change in the fiddler crab, *Uca pugnax. J. Exp. Zool.* 123:29–60.

Brown, F. A., Jr., and H. M. Webb. 1948. Temperature relations of an endogenous daily rhythmicity in the fiddler crab, *Uca. Physiol. Zool.,* 21:371–381.

Fingerman, M. 1955. Persistent daily and tidal rhythms of color change in *Callinectes sapidus. Biol. Bull.,* 109:255–264.

Fingerman, M. 1956. Phase difference in the tidal rhythms of color change of two species of fiddler crab. *Biol. Bull.*, 110:274–290.

Fingerman, M., M. E. Lowe, and W. C. Mobberly, Jr. 1958 Environmental factors involved in setting the phases of tidal rhythm of color change in the fiddler crabs *Uca pugilator* and *Uca minax. Limnol. Oceanogr.*, 3:271–282.

Fingerman, M., R. Nagabhushanam, and L. Philpott. 1961. Physiology of the melanophores in the crab *Sesarma reticulatum. Biol. Bull.*, 120:337–347.

Fingerman, M., and Y. Yamamoto. 1964. Daily rhythm of color change in eyestalkless fiddler crabs, *Uca pugilator. Amer. Zool.*, 4:334.

Hines, M. N. 1954. A tidal rhythm in behavior of melanophores in autotomized legs of *Uca pugnax. Biol. Bull.*, 107:386–396.

Hogben, L. T., and D. Slome. 1931. The pigmentary effector system. VI. The dual character of endocrine coordination in amphibian colour change. *Proc. Roy. Soc. (London), Ser. B*, 108:10–53.

Megušar, F. 1912. Experimente über den Farbwechsel der Crustacean. (I. Gelasimus. II. Potamobius. III. Palaemonetes. IV. Palaemon). *Arch. Entwmech. Org.*, 33:462–665.

Palmer, J. D. 1967. Daily and tidal components in the persistent rhythmic activity of the crab, *Sesarma. Nature*, 215:64–66.

Powell, B. L. 1962a. Chromatophorotropins in the central nervous system of *Carcinus maenas. Crustaceana*, 4:143–150.

Powell, B. L. 1962b. Types, distribution and rhythmical behaviour of the chromatophores of juvenile *Carcinus maenas. J. Anim. Ecol.*, 31:251–261.

Powell, B. L. 1966. The control of the 24 hour rhythm of colour change in juvenile *Carcinus maenas. Proc. R.I.A.*, 64:379–399.

Stephens, G. C. 1962. Circadian melanophore rhythms of the fiddler crab: interation between animals. *Ann. N.Y. Acad. Sci.*, 98:926–939.

Webb, H. M., M. F. Bennett, and F. A. Brown, Jr. 1954. Persistence of an endogenous diurnal rhythmicity in eyestalkless *Uca pugilator. Biol. Bull.*, 106:371–377.

5 Oxygen-Consumption Rhythms

FIDDLER CRABS

The day-to-day pattern of oxygen consumption in the fiddler crabs, *Uca pugnax* and *U. pugilator* was observed in specially designed continuous-recording respirometers (Brown, 1954) in which the reaction vessels were spacious enough to permit running-in-place on the slick concave glass walls (Figure 5-1). A predominant, persistent tidal rhythm (Figure 5-2A), along with a low-amplitude daily component (Figure 5-3), was found in oxygen consumption for both species (Brown, Bennett, and Webb, 1954). The peaks of the tidal cycle in *U. pugnax* corresponded to the times of low tide during the summer months but then transformed into a unimodal lunar-day cycle between mid-November and February and then an inverted bimodal tidal cycle before again adopting the adaptive summer form (Webb and Brown, 1961).

By dividing a sample population in two and recording locomotor activity in one group and oxygen consumption in the other, it was found that the rhythm in the latter was mainly a consequence of the former (Brett, Webb, and Brown, 1959) as the two rhythms were in approximate phase synchrony.

Removal of the eyestalks of *U. pugilator* destroyed the tidal component of the rhythm (Figure 5-2B) but left the daily one undisturbed (Brown *et al.*, 1954).

In follow-up and confirming studies, it was found that both the form and amplitude of the daily rhythm were identical with those of the tidal rhythm during the summers of 1955, 1956, and 1957 (Webb and Brown, 1958) but that the daily component had inverted during the summer of 1954 (Brown, Webb, and Bennett, 1958), in spite of the fact that the crabs were collected from the same mud flat and that the experiments were carried out in the same laboratory. By chance, it was later learned that cosmic-ray physicists were similarly perplexed that summer in that

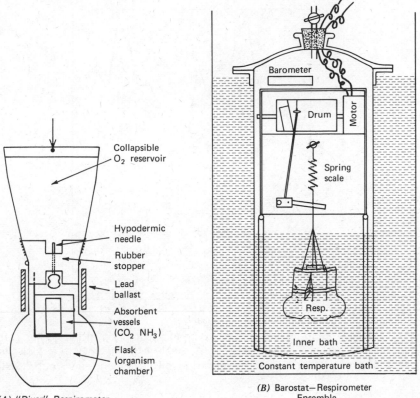

Collapsible
O_2 reservoir

Hypodermic
needle

Rubber
stopper

Lead
ballast

Absorbent
vessels
(CO_2 NH_3)

Flask
(organism
chamber)

Barometer

Drum

Motor

Spring
scale

Resp.

Inner bath

Constant temperature bath

(A) "Diver" Respirometer

(B) Barostat—Respirometer
Ensemble

Figure 5-1. Recording respirometer–barostat assembly. (A) Diver: As an organism, such as a crab, consumes oxygen from the air in the flask, O_2 is replaced from the collapsible reservoir and CO_2 and NH_3 are absorbed by KOH and cupric chloride. The buoyancy of the diver decreases as O_2 is consumed, it sinks, and the sinking rate is recorded on the rotating drum. (B) The divers are maintained in a hermetically sealed barostat in which light, temperature, oxygen tension, carbon dioxide tension, and atmospheric pressure are all held constant (after Brown, 1970).

the mean-daily rhythm in the intensity of primary cosmic radiation had also inverted. Analytical comparisons were made between the crab and radiation rhythms, the results of which are shown in Figure 5-3, and it was found that the two curves mirrored each other to an amazing degree. Whatever the significance of this relationship, it is certainly not a direct one, since most primary radiation does not reach the surface of the earth intact, being altered in collisions with air molecules, and captured by the geomagnetic field. It is the secondary radiation arising from these inter-

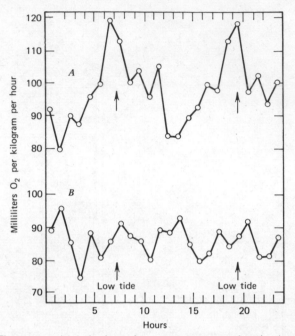

Figure 5-2. The mean tidal rhythm of oxygen consumption in the fiddler crab, *Uca pugilator* in dim LL and 25°C (*A*). As seen in *B,* the rhythm is lost after the crabs' eyestalks have been amputated (Brown, Bennett, and Webb, 1954).

actions that reaches the ground and these derivatives in no simple way represent the rhythmic fluctuations of their primary parents.

In passing, it should be mentioned that studies of the direct effect of cosmic radiation on a biological rhythm have been carried out. As described by the Rossi curve, cosmic-radiation showers are increased by cascade multiplication under thicknesses of lead up to 17 mm; absorption gains the upper hand in plates thicker than this. Using this information, Brown, Bennett, and Ralph (1955) artificially increased the flux of secondary radiation on a sample population of *U. pugnax* with thicknesses of lead varying between 3 and 21 mm. Over a 3-month interval, they followed the color-change rhythm in these crabs in DD, either under lead or sham shields. They found a small, but significant, increase (2-8%) in the amplitude of the pigment-dispersion rhythm under lead during the midday and a similar small decrease during the early morning hours.

Background radiation undergoes a daily rhythm in intensity (Duell, 1954); this and its ability to penetrate into standard constant conditions make it a likely suspect as an exogenous time-giving force—the kind of

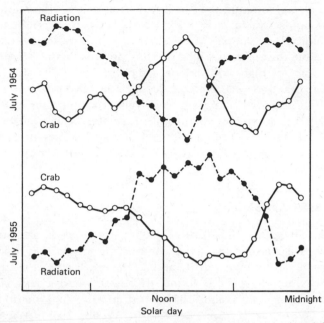

Figure 5-3. Comparison of the mean diurnal variations, calculated for 31-day periods, of the persistent oxygen-consumption rhythm in the fiddler crab, *Uca pugnax* (open points), and the intensity rhythm of primary cosmic radiation (solid points) during July 1954 and 1955. Three-hour moving means used to smooth curves (modified from Brown, Webb, and Bennett, 1958).

geophysical influence sought by advocates of the external-timing hypothesis (Chapter 1). However, the effect produced on the color-change rhythm was only on the amplitude, an alteration that really provides no information on the role of radiation as a time-giver. Only changes in period or phase (or a loss of the wave form in a process still functioning at a normal level) signify an induced alteration at the level of the underlying clock.

GREEN CRABS

Both the rates in gill ventilation (i.e., the rate at which water is pumped through the gill chamber) and oxygen consumption were found to be rhythmic in the green crab, *Carcinus maenas*, by Arudpragasam and Naylor (1964). To isolate the exhalant stream of the respiratory current, a polythene hood was fixed over the anterior end of the crab and held in place by a rubber band. Water funneled into the hood was channeled into a reservoir, and the overflow was measured automatically by a periodic-siphon-activated pen (Figure 5-4). Oxygen determinations were made periodically in samples of exhalant and fresh water collected simultaneously from the apparatus. The rhythms found (Figure 5-5) peaked just after the times of high tide and persisted for 5 days in LL (dim) and 16°C. Since the crab was tethered during the observations, it was concluded that the periodic increase in oxygen consumption could not be attributed to the locomotor rhythm—in fact, the latter was out of phase with peaks in O₂ consumption. Therefore, peak times of oxygen consumption must have been caused by increases in ventilation movements and general metabolism.

OTHER ORGANISMS

Sandeen, Stephens, and Brown (1954) reported a persistent tidal rhythm, with a concomitant daily component, in the gastropods: *Urosalpinx cinereus*, the oyster drill; and *Littorina litorea*, the periwinkle. Identical rhythms have been found in the seaweed *Fucus vesiculosus* (Brown, Sandeen, and Webb, 1954), and in the mud snail, *Nassarius* (*Ilyanassa*) *obsoletus* (Brown, Brett, and Webb, 1958). Wieser (1962) reports a tidal rhythm in oxygen consumption in the isopod *Naesa bidentata* that persists for only 2 days in CC.

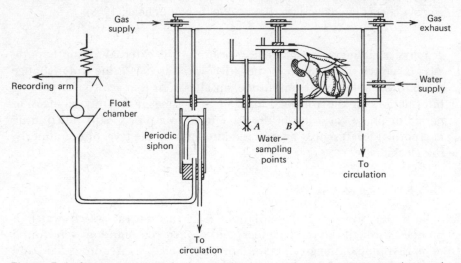

Figure 5-4. Apparatus used for measuring rates of oxygen consumption and gill ventilation in the green crab, *Carcinus maenas*. See text for a description of its mode of function (Arudpragasam and Naylor, 1963).

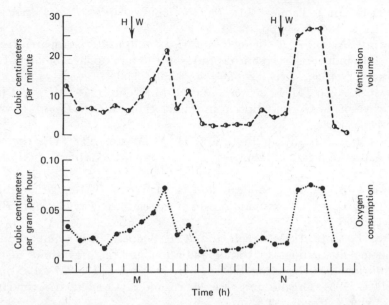

Figure 5-5. The gill-ventilation and oxygen-consumption rhythms in the green crab, *Carcinus maenas*, in LL and 16°C. HW represents midpoints of high tide (modified from Arudpragasam and Naylor, 1963).

A rather unusual tidal rhythm in metabolism has been reported by Pamatmat (1968), who studied an entire benthic community! Large sediment samples from a West Coast sandflat were brought into the laboratory and maintained in LL, TT, and away from the tide. Periodic measurements of the oxygen consumption of the intact infauna revealed that the rates over 2 days in CC were highest at the times of high tide.

Literature Cited

Arudpragasam, K. D., and E. Naylor. 1964. Gill ventilation volumes, oxygen consumption and respiratory rhythms in *Carcinus maenas*. *J. Exp. Biol.*, 41:309–321.

Brett, W. J., H. M. Webb, and F. A. Brown, Jr. 1959. Contribution of locomotion to the oxygen-consumption rhythm in *Uca pugnax*. *Biol. Bull.*, 117:405.

Brown, F. A., Jr. 1954. A simple, automatic, continuous-recording respirometer. *Rev. Sci. Instrum.*, 25:415–417.

Brown, F. A., Jr., 1970. Hypothesis of environmental timing of the clock. In J. Palmer, Ed., *The Biological Clock: Two Views*. Academic, New York, pp. 13–59.

Brown, F. A., Jr., M. F. Bennett, and C. L. Ralph. 1955. Apparent reversible influence of cosmic-ray-induced showers upon a biological system. *Proc. Soc. Exper. Biol. Med.*, 89:332–338.

Brown, F. A., Jr., M. F. Bennett, and H. M. Webb. 1954. Daily and tidal rhythms of O_2-consumption in fiddler crabs. *J. Cell. Comp. Physiol.*, 44:477–506.

Brown, F. A., Jr., W. J. Brett, and H. M. Webb. 1958. The rhythmic nature of metabolism in *Ilyanassa* in constant conditions. *Biol. Bull.*, 115:345.

Brown, F. A., Jr., M. I. Sandeen, and H. M. Webb. 1954. Solar and lunar rhythms of O_2-consumption in the seaweed, *Fucus*. *Biol. Bull.*, 107:306.

Brown, F. A., Jr., H. M. Webb, and M. F. Bennett, 1958. Comparisons of some fluctuations in cosmic radiation and in organismic activity during 1954, 1955 and 1956. *Amer. J. Physiol.*, 195:237–243.

Duell, G. 1954. Organic responses to cosmic rays and their secondaries. *Meterol. Monogr.*, 2:61–67.

Pamatmat, M. M. 1968. Ecology and metabolism of a benthic community on an intertidal sandflat. *Int. Rev. Ges. Hydrobiol.*, 53:211–298.

Sandeen, M. I., G. C. Stephens, and F. A. Brown, Jr. 1954. Persistent daily and tidal rhythms of O_2 consumption in two species of marine snails. *Physiol. Zool.*, 27:350–356.

Webb, H. M., and F. A. Brown, Jr. 1958. The repetition of pattern in the respiration of *Uca pugnax*. *Biol. Bull.*, 115:303–318.

Webb, H. M., and F. A. Brown, Jr. 1961. Seasonal variations in O_2-consumption of *Uca pugnax*. *Biol. Bull.*, 121:561–571.

Weiser, W. 1962. Adaptations of two intertidal isopods. I. Respiration and feeding in *Naesa bidentata*. *J. mar. biol. Ass. U.K.* 42:665-682.

6 Translocation Experiments

The persistence of the phase of a tidal rhythm after translocation across major time zones and then during the maintenance of the test organisms in CC has been examined by only a few investigators. The usual reason for undertaking such observations is to test for the permeation into the laboratory of some rhythmic geophysical force(s) whose phase is longitude-dependent. The nonescapement-clock hypothesis depends on the involvement of these forces, and protagonists and antagonists of this hypothesis have used post translocation response in CC as a way of examining its validity. An immediately obvious geophysical parameter that might act as such a force is lunar gravitation, whose influence on the physical environment of the earth is quite striking: in addition to its well-known influence on oceanic tides, the surface of the land is raised and dropped as much as 50 cm each time the moon passes overhead (Berger and Lovberg, 1970; Kuo, Jachens, Ewing, and White, 1970).

The filtration-rate rhythm (Figure 2–21) of the mussel, *Mytilus*, was one of the first to be studied after a cross-country translocation. The shellfish were collected on the Massachusetts coast and shipped rapidly—in CC—to California. Still maintained in CC, the pumping rhythm was found to persist and displayed the East Coast phase during a 4-week sojourn in the laboratory. Subsequent to this, a 1-week exposure in cages to the California tides brought about a persistent phase change to that habitat (Rao, 1954). Unfortunately, the one attempt to confirm this work by Pickens (as cited in Enright, 1963) failed, even though the same measuring apparatus (and a more refined version) was used. In fact, in CC, water-propulsion rates were found to be arrhythmic.

In another translocation experiment, fiddler crabs (*Uca pugnax*) collected in Massachusetts were placed into two wooden buckets, one of which was flown overnight to California. Both were opened simultaneously the following day in identical CC, and the color-change rhythms of both groups quantified for the next 6 days. The flight across 3½ time zones seemed to have advanced both the daily and tidal peaks of the

California-housed crabs by 22 min, but otherwise both populations retained a constant phase relationship (Brown, Webb, and Bennett, 1955).

Brown (1954) examined the effect of translocation on the shell-gaping rhythm of the oyster (*Ostrea*). These bivalves were shipped nearly 900 miles, from Connecticut to Illinois, and maintained in CC for the next 45 days. A form estimate curve (Figure 6-1) for the first 15 days in CC showed that the animals retained the phase of their Connecticut habitat through these days. The peaks in the next 15-day composite curve were delayed 3 h, and it was concluded that the curve for the last 15 days showed no phase change. It was emphasized that the single phase change brought the organisms into approximate synchrony with times of maximum lunar gravitational attraction in Illinois (i.e., to the times at which

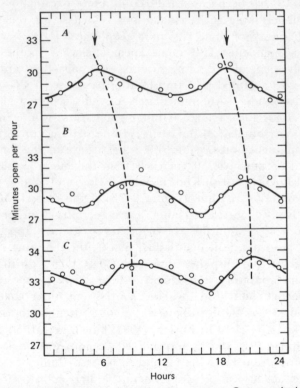

Figure 6-1. The shell-gaping rhythm in the oyster, *Ostrea virginica*. Curves are average daily pattern of 15 oysters in LL (<0.1 ft.-c). (*A*) Pattern for the first 15 days in CC after transport from Connecticut to Illinois. (*B*) Same for next 15 days in Illinois. (*C*) Same for last 15 days. Falling arrows indicate midpoints of high tide in Connecticut (Brown, 1955).

high tides might be expected). This suggests that the organisms had become entrained to some force that is associated with the upper and lower transits of the moon and is able to permeate standard laboratory CC.

An alternate interpretation is also possible. Because of the mode of data collection, the smallest units of data for which the tidal component could be extracted were 15-day segments. Even with this lumping, it is quite obvious that a pronounced phase delay had resulted during the second 15 days of the study. Interpretation of the curve representing the last 15 days is more difficult: the animals had been in CC for over a month and the peaks had broadened—and to me, it appears that some additional phase delay has actually taken place, albeit not anywhere near as great as that in the preceding two week period. Therefore, it is questionable whether the phase changes represent entrainment to a moon-related force: they may simply be the manifestation of a circatidal rhythm, in which the period becomes slightly longer than 12.4 h during the second two weeks of incarceration but more nearly tidal during the last two weeks. Enright (1965) has reanalyzed these data and claims that the tidal rhythm reported is an artifact.

Bennett (1963) has reported a curious phase alteration in the spontaneous locomotor rhythm of the fiddler crab, *U. pugnax*. She collected crabs from two beaches not more than 6 miles apart but whose tides differed by roughly 4 h because of differences in topography. The crabs were placed individually in actographs and maintained in LL (0.2 lux) and a relatively constant temperature. On the first day after capture the rhythms of both groups displayed the approximate phase relations of their old beach habitat and were therefore about 4 h out of phase with one another (Figure 6-2A). During the next 7 days one group systematically altered its phase and came into synchrony with the other group (Figure 6-2B). This phase appeared to hold for the remainder of the observations—5 more days (Figure 6-2C)—and was in approximate synchrony with upper and lower transits of the moon. The experiment was repeated a second time with the same results. These data certainly suggest that while the local tidal schedule obviously sets the phase in the habitat, in the absence of the tides the phase is determined in some other way, possibly by primary lunar events.

By way of comparison, it should be emphasized that the color-change rhythm of the same species, collected from these same two locations, and studied in CC in the same laboratory, retained the phase of tidal events on their native beaches during 18 days of study in CC (Brown, Fingerman, Sandeen, and Webb, 1953). This certainly complicates the interpretation of the results obtained with the activity rhythm.

The only other translocation study carried out in which the test organ-

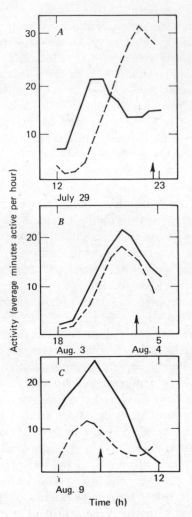

Figure 6-2. The persistent tidal activity rhythms of two populations of fiddler crabs (*Uca pugnax*) in LL (0.2 lux). The sample represented by the solid line was collected from a beach on Cape Cod, Mass.; the other animals (dashed line) were collected from Martha's Vineyard, Mass. The tides at the two collection sites differ by approximately 4 h (the times of the mid low tides on the Cape Cod beach are represented by the arrows). Each curve is the average of 8 crabs, each of which was maintained in its own actograph, and represents only one tidal peak of the rhythm. *A,* Phase relationship on first day after capture; *B,* the phase synchrony by day 7; *C,* the approximate phase retention after 5 more days in CC (modified from Bennett, 1963).

72

isms were maintained in CC throughout, was done on an organism—the bee—that displayed only a circadian rhythm. Bee-attracting nectar emanates from flowers only at certain times of day; in fact, this rhythm was shown to be clock-controlled many years ago (Kleber, 1935). Once nectar production begins in the mature flower, the bees soon learn to forage only at these times of secretion each day, and as first shown by Beling (1929), this behavior is also under the control of the biological clock.

While the early work was mostly done in the field, nowadays training rooms built within the confines of the laboratory are used. Each contains a test hive and a feeding station. Sugar water is offered at the latter at only one time each day, and the bees soon learn to come to the station only at this time. Since the light and temperature in the room is held constant, the correct hour is being signaled by the bee's biological clock.

To test for the possibility of celestial influence on the bee clock, identical training rooms were constructed in Paris and New York. These two cities are separated by 76° of longitude and a 5-h difference in time. Forty bees were trained to feed between 8:15 P.M. and 10:15 P.M. in constant conditions in Paris and, after the last training period, were packed up and flown overnight to the matching room in New York. Still maintained in CC, the bees began feeding at their usual Paris time (between 3:15 P.M. and 5:15 P.M. New York time), rather than 8:15 P.M. in New York. A reciprocal experiment was performed with training in New York preceding translocation back to Paris: the results were similar (Renner, 1960). These results suggest that a time-cuing geophysical variable is not involved with the setting of the clock.

SUMMARY AND CONCLUSIONS

No clear-cut pattern emerges from the results detailed above. The long-term study with mussels showed no change of phase, but the one attempt to repeat any aspect of this study failed. The oyster appeared to adopt a new phase, one logically expected if a pervasive, rhythm-influencing environmental force was involved, but an alternate interpretation of these data is also possible. In two different experiments, the fiddler-crab color-change rhythm was unaffected by translocation, but the activity rhythm did abandon the phase of the old habitat and "lock in" to the time of lunar nadir and zenith. The latter finding was repeatable. The bee experiment produced no phase change, but only one day of observation was made at the new longitude.

Therefore, no generalization comes forth from the work done to date, but sufficient evidence is present to at least encourage further work.

Literature Cited

Beling, I. 1929. Über das Zeitgedächtinis der Bienen. *Z. vergl. Physiol.*, 9:259–338.

Bennett, M. F. 1963. The phasing of the cycle of motor activity in the fiddler crab, *Uca pugnax. Z. vergl. Physiol.*, 47:431–437.

Berger, J., and R. H. Lovberg. 1970. Earth strain measurements with a laser interferometer. *Science*, 170:296–303.

Brown, F. A., Jr. 1954. Persistent activity rhythms in the oyster. *Amer. J. Physiol.*, 178:510–514.

Brown, F. A., Jr., M. Fingerman, M. Sandeen, and H. M. Webb. 1953. Persistent diurnal and tidal rhythms of color change in the fiddler crab, *Uca pugnax. J. Exp. Zool.*, 123:29–60.

Brown, F. A., Jr., H. M. Webb, and M. F. Bennett. 1955. Proof for an endogenous component in persistent solar and lunar rhythmicity in organisms. *Proc. Nat. Acad. Sci.*, 41:93–100.

Enright, J. T. 1963. The tidal rhythm of activity of a sand-beach amphipod. *Z. vergl. Physiol.*, 46:276–313.

Enright, J. T. 1965. The search for rhythmicity in biological time-series. *J. Theoret. Biol.*, 8:426–468.

Kleber, E. 1935. Hat des Zeitgedächtnis der Bienen biologische Bedeutung? *Z. vergl. Physiol.*, 22:221–261.

Kuo, J. T., R. C. Jachens, M. Ewing, and G. White. 1970. Transcontinental tidal gravity across the United States. *Science*, 168:968–971.

Rao, K. P. 1954. Tidal rhythmicity of rate of water propulsion in *Mytilus*, and its modifiability by transplantation. *Biol. Bull.*, 106:353–359.

Renner, M. 1960. The contribution of the honey bee to the study of time-sense and astronomical orientation. *Cold Spring Harbor Symp. Quant. Biol.*, 25:361–367.

7 Determination of Phase

THE LOCAL HABITAT

The phase of a tidal rhythm is obviously set by the tides at the particular beach on which an organism dwells; this has been shown, for example, by the work of Brown, Sandeen, and Fingerman (1952), Barnwell (1968), and others, and was discussed in Chapter 2. Phase lability of tidal rhythms is very important, since the times of the tides may vary considerably over relatively short lateral distances of coastline. While adult intertidal organisms may not emigrate widely, their larvae, during the planktonic dispersal stage, often come ashore many miles from the home coastlines of their parents and are thus subjected to tidal cycles temporally quite different from that of their kin.

Also, the tidal rhythm of a single species may differ in phase not only as a function of horizontal distribution along a coastline but also in relation to the animal's vertical position on a single beach. For example, in a series of papers, Fingerman (1956, 1957) and Fingerman, Lowe and Mobberly (1958) demonstrated that the phase of the color-change rhythm of *Uca pugilator* is set by the receding tide: crabs living in burrows at the upper regions of the tidal zone emerge and show maximum pigment dispersion before those of the lower shorelines. Barnwell and Brown (1963) have reported the same high- and low-beach phase differences in *U. pugnax* and *U. pugilator* oxygen-consumption rhythms.

In addition to the entraining role of local tides, in several cases it has been established that unless a member of a species known to display tidal rhythms is exposed to periodic tidal inundation, this rhythm may not be expressed. For example, Altevogt (1959) found that *U. tangeri* living on the margins of a nontidal pool conformed to a daily schedule, while fellow crabs from a nearby intertidal zone displayed tidal rhythms. Green crabs from nontidal habitats in the Irish Sea display only circadian periods in the lab (Naylor, 1960).

The obvious question is then, what physiochemical aspects of the tides produce the actual entrainment? Among the possibilities are periodic immersion, mechanical agitation (i.e., wave action), hydrostatic pressure, chemical changes (including changes in availability of oxygen), temperature, and light–dark cycles.

INUNDATION

Williams and Naylor (1969) examined the role of immersion in phasesetting in the green crab, *Carcinus*. They began with field studies in which "dock crabs" (i.e., crabs not possessing tidal rhythms when brought in from the field) were translocated to cages in either the midtide level of the shoreline, where they were periodically inundated, or below the lowtide level, where they remained permanently submerged. In the latter case the crabs were subjected to the tidal alterations in pressure created by the changing height of the column of water over them and the other physical and chemical changes delivered with each high tide. They re-. mained in these locations for 2–11 days and were then moved to actographs and CC in the laboratory. Both groups displayed equally distinct tidal rhythms, the phase being that of the tide to which they had just been exposed. Therefore, periodic exposure to air appears to induce and set the phase of the rhythm (but see below) but is obviously not a necessity, as shown by the crabs exposed subtidally. To test the specific role of exposure, shore crabs were maintained for 5 days in 12.4-h immersion cycles (6.2 h in air and 6.2 h under seawater) which were offered out of phase with their normal rhythm. Both air and water temperatures were maintained at 19°C. During the immersion portion of each cycle the crabs were active but were quiescent during the exposed periods (Figure 7-1). On the sixth day the cycles were stopped and the crabs maintained in moist air (19°C) for the next few days. No lasting effect of the immersion cycle was noted; in fact, the crabs were arrhythmic.

Enright (1965) and Jones and Naylor (1970), while trying to manipulate the phase of the activity rhythms of the isopods *Excirolana* and *Eurydice*, also found that cycles of submergence and exposure in the lab in TT lacked an entraining effect.

Webb (1972) found that she could increase the longevity of her fiddler crabs, *U. pugnax*, by occasionally changing the water in their actographs. In addition, the replacement of old water with new caused a short burst of activity, showing that the alteration could function as a powerful stimulus of locomotory behavior. Taking her cue from this response, Webb went on to test the entraining effectiveness of water changes by offering them at 24.8-h, 24.0-h, and irregular intervals for up to 14 consecutive

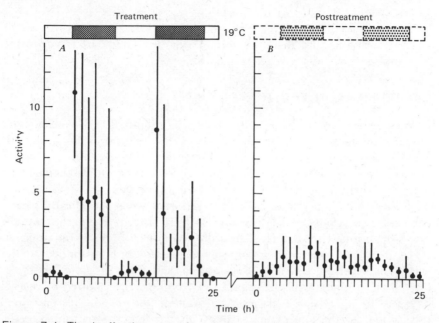

Figure 7-1. The ineffectiveness of periodic inundation as an entraining agent of the green crab (*Carcinus maenas*) activity rhythm. *A*. Form-estimate curve for crabs exposed to 5 days of cycles of 6.2 h of immersion in water alternating with 6.2 h exposure to air; both air and water temperatures were held constant at 19°C. *B*. Form-estimate curve for 3 days posttreatment in 19°C moist air. Black bars signify times of immersion, and stippled bars, "expected immersions." Points are means of 5 crabs, and vertical skewers signify range of responses (Williams and Naylor, 1969).

days to crabs maintained under LL (10 ft-c) or LD 15:9 (10 ft-c). In all cases—as expected—a short burst of activity followed each water change, but in no way was the tidal activity rhythm entrained by the stimulus; instead, the treatment simply inserted an additional peak into the data, but it disappeared on removal of the stimulus.

In fact, thus far, rather surprisingly, the only reports in which inundation had even a quasi-entraining effect is on the vertical-migration rhythms of the diatoms *Hantzschia* and *Surirella*. In the former, it was found that in the field, retention of water within a temporarily erected dam prevented the diatoms from emerging at low tide and that artificial flooding forced them down (Palmer, 1960). In a lab population, *Surirella* was forced to burrow by flooding, and this single treatment set the phase of burrowing on the next day but not for subsequent days (Hopkins, 1966). These results, however, are probably peculiar only to this type of migratory rhythm and therefore should not be thought of as beginning contributions toward a new generalization.

MECHANICAL AGITATION

As described earlier, the isopod, *Excirolana* (Figure 2-17), swims activity only during the peaks of high tide; at ebb it buries itself in the sand. This activity is displayed in CC as a persistent activity rhythm. In nature the animals appear to be stimulated to action by the ascent of the pounding surf during flood tide. Therefore, in the lab, "wave simulators" were contrived simply from columnar jars that were periodically stirred with sufficient vigor so that the resulting maelstrom swept the animals into suspension. The standard agitation cycle was 6 h of stirring alternating with 6 h of quietude. In some experiments sand was added to the water; in others it was not. Two and a half days of agitation cycles offered out of phase with the organism's rhythm were followed by several days in CC, where phase changes were noted. Both conditions entrained the isopods to the approximate times of swirling, the treatment being more effective if sand was included (Figure 7-2). Perhaps the sand intensified the mechanical stimulation. The entraining effectiveness of other environmental variables was also tested: cyclic chemical regimes, feeding, and oxygen tensions were tried but found to be ineffective (Enright, 1965). Apparently, mechanical agitation is the dominant entraining component in the environment of *Excirolana*.

As described in Chapter 2, the form of this animal's rhythm in the lab is determined by the tide to which it was exposed just prior to capture. Learning from Enright's work that it was the mechanical agitation of the tide that set the phase of the rhythm, a series of experiments were undertaken by Klapow (1972) to learn the subtleties of its role on the form and amplitude of the laboratory-expressed rhythm. First, using a population that had been maintained in the laboratory for 26 days and that had therefore become arrhythmic, he subjected them to two 1.5-h intervals of swirling, spaced 12.5 h apart. This simple treatment caused the tidal rhythm to burgeon again (Figure 7-3).

This success provided the impetus for more elaborate wave-simulator manipulations. The crustaceans were collected and divided into 2 populations of 115 isopods each. Group A was then subjected to 7 days of periodic agitation consisting of 30 min of swirling each afternoon and 120-min periods of the same in the morning; the two treatments were

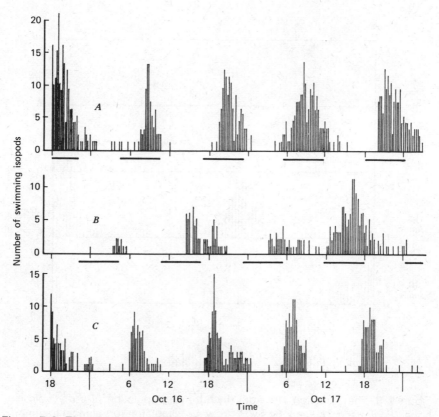

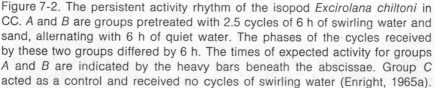

Figure 7-2. The persistent activity rhythm of the isopod *Excirolana chiltoni* in CC. *A* and *B* are groups pretreated with 2.5 cycles of 6 h of swirling water and sand, alternating with 6 h of quiet water. The phases of the cycles received by these two groups differed by 6 h. The times of expected activity for groups *A* and *B* are indicated by the heavy bars beneath the abscissae. Group *C* acted as a control and received no cycles of swirling water (Enright, 1965a).

separated from one another by 12.5 h (Figure 7-4A). Population B received the same cycles except that the 30-min intervals of wave simulation were offered in the mornings. These agitation cycles were designed to mimic the tidal semidiurnal inequality (Figure 1-9) encountered on some days on the shoreline. As clearly shown in Figure 7-4, the treatments not only entrained the animals' rhythms, they also produced an inequality in amplitude.

Wave action was found to be an important entraining agent of the

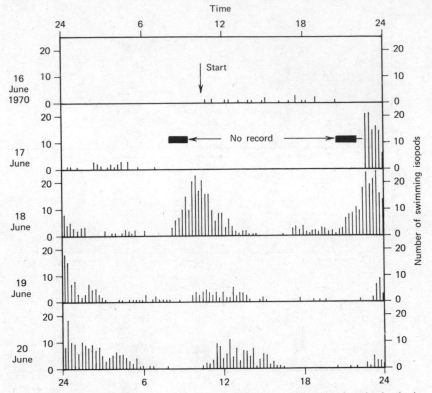

Figure 7-3. The induction of a tidal rhythm in a population of arrhythmic isopods (*Excirolana chiltoni*) by two 2-h wave-simulator turbulence treatments
(signified by solid horizontal bars) (modified from Klapow, 1972).

identical rhythm in another sand-dwelling isopod, *Eurydice*, as was demonstrated by Jones and Naylor (1970). These investigators set up slightly
different agitation cycles than Enright and Klapow had used: offering
only 30 min of stirring at 12-h intervals. In one experiment they subjected their arrhythmic animals to only one 1-h interval of agitation, and
even this brief, aperiodic stimulus induced a quasi-tidal periodicity.

On the other hand, mechanical stimulation did not initiate rhythmic
activity and entrain it in the prawn, *Palaemon*. Rodriguez and Naylor
(1972) subjected arrhythmic animals to cycles of 6 h of running water
alternating with 6 h of standing water (the temperature was not given,
but presumably it was constant at 15° or 18°C) for 10 days. The animals
were less active during the standing-water phase, but this pattern did
not persist in CC.

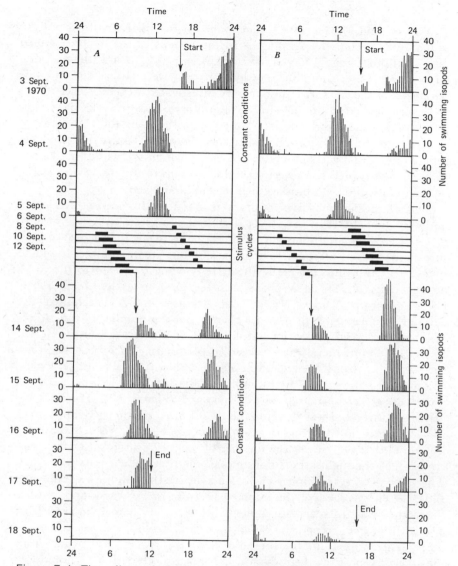

Figure 7-4. The effect of alternating long and short agitation stimuli on the entrainment and form of the persistent activity rhythm of *Excirolana chiltoni*. Alternating at 12.5-h intervals, a 2-h or ½-h interval of swirling (solid horizontal bars) was offered (in reverse order in *A* and *B*) to two populations of isopods. Seven days of treatment not only set the phase of the rhythms, it also established an inequality in the amplitude of the alternating peaks when the animals were returned to CC (Klapow, 1972).

PRESSURE

Williams and Naylor (1969) had found that a tidal rhythm could be induced in *Carcinus* by keeping arrhythmic crabs constantly submerged in a light-proof cage (Naylor and Atkinson, 1972) below the low-tide level of the Wales shoreline. Pressure changes were suspected, and this parameter of the tides was subsequently investigated. Several clever means have been devised to produce in the laboratory, pressure cycles of various forms, amplitudes, and periods. Most are brilliant in the simplicity of their design; for example, the apparatus shown in Figure 7-5 produces reliable sinusoidal pressure cycles in a closed container, while that shown in Figure 7-6 is used to subject several organisms to square-wave pressure oscillations, while maintaining them in running water.

Some of the first positive results were obtained by Naylor, Atkinson, and Williams (1971), who subjected arrhythmic green crabs to pressure cycles of 6.2 h at atmospheric pressure, alternating with 6.2 h at a pressure equal to 3 m of water. Three days of this treatment was found to induce a rhythm into the crabs, the activity being restricted to the times of high pressure. The new phase persisted for four cycles. In more detailed follow-up studies, Naylor and Atkinson (1972) examined the effect of the magnitude of pressure change and the number of repetitions of a pressure cycle needed for entrainment. In CC, crabs were subjected to four different square wave cycles of pressure (in which peak test pressures were 0.1, 0.2, 0.3, or 0.6 atm above ambient for six "tidal" cycles. All entrained the crabs equally well and the induced rhythms persisted for six cycles in constant pressure afterward (Figure 7-7). The pressure increment threshold was therefore below 0.1 atm. When arrhythmic crabs were subjected to from one to seven pressure cycles of 0.3 or 0.6 atm, it was found that the greater the number of repetitions, the better the "precision" (i.e., the higher the amplitude) of the rhythm after change to CC. The response was rectilinear. Two other interesting findings were made. First, the effectiveness of the imposed pressure cycles was found to be a function of time of year, entrainment being best in September and least evident in March. Second, for September data, while the peaks developed during entrainment to pressure did not vary systematically one from the other, the posttreatment data in CC showed alternating high and low peaks in the persisting rhythms (Figure 7-7). The significance of this will be discussed in Chapter 10.

The remainder of the reports on the use of pressure cycles are either ambiguous or negative. Morgan (1965), studying the activity rhythm of an amphipod, *Corophium*, found that pressure cycles mimicking the tides in amplitude and period (consisting of gradually increasing pres-

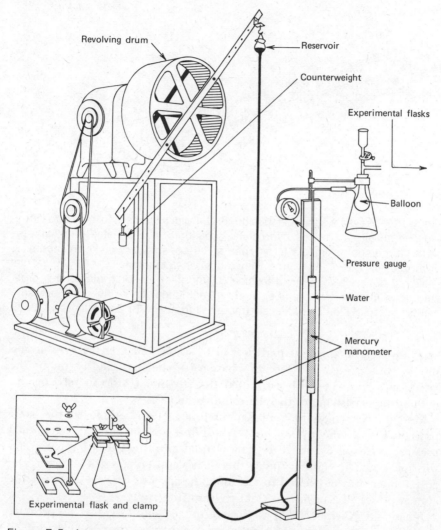

Figure 7-5. Apparatus used to produce sinusoidal tidal cycles of pressure change. The slowly rotating arm raises and lowers a column of mercury, and the changing weight is transferred to a column of water and then to an experimental flask (inset). A partially collapsed rubber balloon isolates the column from the experimental flasks. A range of pressure changes can be produced by hanging the manometer reservoir from different holes along the rotating bar (Morgan, Nelson-Smith, and Knight-Jones, 1964).

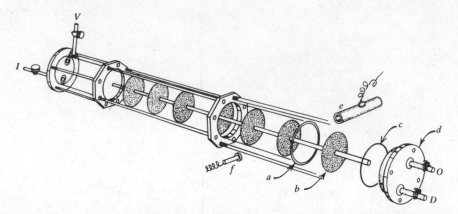

Figure 7-6. Pressure chamber designed to hold 8 crabs and measure spontaneous activity at various hydrostatic pressures in a constant flow of seawater: *a*, perspex cylinder; *b*, perspex discs separating animal chambers; *c*, O-ring; *d*, cap; *e*, light source with red filter; *f*, photocell; *D*, drain; *I*, inlet valve; *O*, outlet valve; *V*, vent to clear cylinder of air. Saltwater under pressure flows through the chamber, and by restricting the outflow, the pressure can be increased to desired levels (modified from Naylor and Atkinson, 1972).

sures up to a maximum equal to 8 m of water and then back to atmospheric), but offered 180° out of phase with the natural rhythm of the organism, almost instantly entrained the rhythm. Unfortunately, he did not test the persistence of the phase change in CC.

Morgan, Nelson-Smith, and Knight-Jones (1964) employed the same procedure with the pycnogonid, *Nymphon gracile*, and also included pressure cycles of 8 and 16 h. The animal entrained to all three cycles with peak activity falling under the early "ebb" of pressure. Again, the entrainment was not tested in CC, nor, in fact, was it even known if the animal possessed a persistent tidal rhythm in activity.

Jones and Naylor (1970) subjected the isopod *Eurydice* to pressure cycles consisting of a pressure equal to 5 m of water every 30 sec for 30 min at 12-h intervals for 4 days. The treatment appeared to establish a tidal rhythm in previously arrhythmic animals; however, the established phase bore no adaptive association with the high-pressure portion of the pretreatments. Morgan (1973) demonstrated that *Eurydice* activity can be made to mimic very short sinusoidal pressure cycles. Enright (1962) had demonstrated that a very slight pressure increase would stimulate *Synchelidium* (but not *Excirolana*) to activity. This finding encouraged the belief that tidal pressure might be a dominant zeitgeber in this amphipod's life. However, by sealing populations in flexible bottles

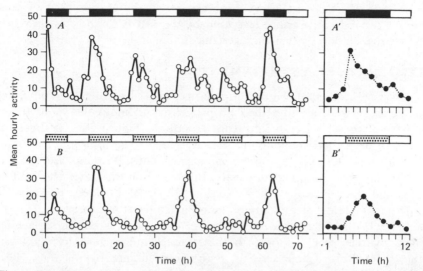

Figure 7-7. The induction of a tidal activity rhythm by pressure cycles. *A*, mean hourly activity of 6 arrhythmic green crabs (*Carcinus maenas*) subjected to pressure cycles of 6 hours at ambient atmospheric pressure, alternating with 6 hours of ambient plus 0.6 atm (signified by overhead horizontal dark bars); *A'*, the form-estimate curve for the 3 days; *B*, the instilled persistent rhythm at constant atmospheric pressure (stippling signifies the times of "expected pressure increase"). Note that in *B* a semidiurnal inequality in amplitude has arisen spontaneously (Naylor and Atkinson, 1972).

anchored to the sea bottom, he showed that this was not the case. The bottles, because of their easily deformable sides, transferred tidal pressures on to the incarcerated animals but isolated them from chemical change. The populations within the bottles displayed a phase different from the tide. Also ineffective was a laboratory offering of a sinusoidal pressure change that mimicked in amplitude the pressure changes of the local tides (but with a 12-h period) (Enright, 1963).

Gibson (1971) subjected the littoral fish *Blennius* to natural pressure changes by anchoring aquaria 5-7 ft below the high-tide level for 5-, 10-, and 20-day intervals. Control fish were maintained in adjacent aquaria attached to a floating dock. Fish that had become arrhythmic after storage in the lab for 6 weeks and fish that were from a distant shore where the tides differed in phase by several hours were both used. Entrainment in the experimentals was suggested after 5 days and was well established and persisted in CC after 20 days. Since it had previously been shown that cycles in temperature, light, agitation, and feeding had no entraining effect on the fish, Gibson attributed the entrainment to pressure. The mode of pressure reception by the fish is unknown—they lose their swim bladders when they metamorphose from the larval stage.

TEMPERATURE ENTRAINMENT

It was mentioned above that inundation cycles in which air and water temperature were identical had no propensity to mold the spontaneous activity of the green crab into a tidal pattern (Figure 7-1). (Palmer, in unpublished experiments, found the same to be true for *U. pugnax* and *Sesarma reticulatum*.) In subsequent experiments, Williams and Naylor (1969) repeated the procedure again, but this time the water was held at 13°C and the air temperature at either 17° or 24°C, depending on the experiment. These treatments provided a temperature differential of 4° or 11°C. In the 5 days during which the "dock crabs" (i.e., those lacking tidal rhythms) were exposed to these compound cycles, the crabs entrained, confining their activity to the cool submerged portions. This phase relation persisted for 3 days when the crabs were removed to CC.

The experiment was repeated again, but this time the immersion cycle was omitted: 6.2 h of 13°C alternating with 6.2 h of 17° or 24°C were used. The dock crabs synchronized their activity peaks to the 13° segment during the 5 days of treatment, but this entrained phase persisted in CC only in the group from the cycle offering the 11° differential (Figure 7-8).

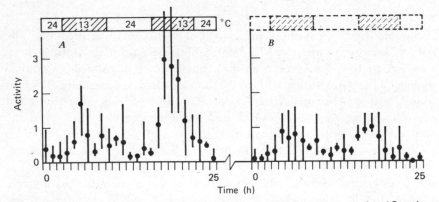

Figure 7-8. The induction of a tidal activity rhythm in green crabs (*Carcinus maenas*) by temperature cycles. *A*, form-estimate curve of activity for 5 days in 6.2-h periods of 13°C alternating with 6.2-h intervals at 24°C; *B*, average curve for 3 days posttreatment at 13°C. Points are means of 5 crabs, and vertical skewers signify range of responses (modified from Williams and Naylor, 1969).

Therefore, in *Carcinus,* it is the drop in temperature (and the increase in pressure) delivered by the flood tide that sets the rhythm to the local beach situation. Immersion enhances the temperature effect (since entrainment was accomplished by the 4° temperature differential combined with cyclic immersion), possibly by improving heat transfer.

Enright (1965) did not examine the possible entraining role of temperature cycles on *Excirolana* but states elsewhere (1963) that it would be a particularly unreliable zeitgeber in this animal's habitat, for temperatures fluctuate through several degrees independent of the tides because of irregular mixing of water in the surf and changes caused by cloud and fog cover. He has shown (1963), however, that somewhat extreme temperature pulses (some lasting as long as 24 h up or down will cause phase delays (only).

Jones and Naylor (1970) also did not subject the *Eurydice* activity rhythm to temperature cycles, although cold pulses are known to rephase the rhythm.

Gibson (1971) provided the fish *Blennius* with 12-h temperature cycles (6 h of 3°C alternating with 6 h of 13°C) for 5–20 days and found that the treatment had no entraining effect.

LIGHT ENTRAINMENT

A universal characteristic of circadian rhythms is their resetability (i.e., phase lability) and entrainability (Figure 7-9) by light pulses and LD cycles (for review, see Wilkins, 1960; Hastings, 1964). Because so many other properties are shared between circadian and tidal rhythms, a priori one might expect entrainment by light to be included in the list also. On the other hand, it would be self-destructive for a *tidal* rhythm to allow itself to be entrained by *daily* LD changes. However, 12.4-h LD cycle might be effective, for—at least during the daytime and on moonlit nights—an intertidal organism that spends part of each tide buried in the substratum or under beach wrack imposes a quasi-tidal LD cycle on itself while performing its tidal rituals. In the laboratory, tidal rhythms have been subjected to both daily and tidal LD cycles with the following results.

In these studies, it has been found that tidal rhythms persist unaltered in LD 12:12 and in natural LD cycles. This has been demonstrated for rhythms in activity in *Uca* (Figure 2-11) (Webb and Brown, 1965; Barnwell, 1968; Webb, 1971), *Carcinus* (Naylor, 1960), *Sesarma* (Palmer, unpublished), *Eurydice* (Jones and Naylor, 1970), and *Blennius* (Gibson, 1971); in color change in *Uca* (Webb, 1966), and in vertical migrations in *Hantzschia* (Figure 3-3) (Palmer and Round, 1967) and others.

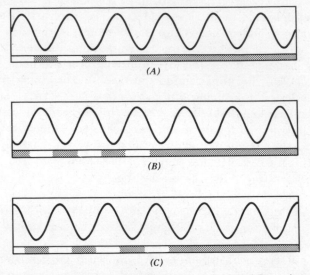

Figure 7-9. The entrainment of a typical daily rhythm by LD cycles. In each of the three cases above, the rhythm is subjected to LD 12:12 cycles, each of the last two being 8 h out of phase with the one above it. The peaks of the rhythm become entrained to the interval of "light on," and this phase then persists when the lighting regimen is changed to DD.

Barnwell (1966) has made the very interesting observation (which will be discussed further in Chapter 10) that LD 12:12 keeps the tidal activity rhythms of the fiddler crab at a strict 12.4-h period (Figure 2-7), while in CC the rhythm becomes circatial (Figure 2-8).

The results obtained in experiments employing LD cycles with approximate tidal frequencies are about the same. For example, Enright (1965) subjected the isopod, *Excirolana*, to LD 6:6 (20 lux) for 2½ days timed to conflict with the existing phase of the animal's persistent activity rhythm. When the isopods were subsequently observed in CC, no phase entrainment was apparent. The persistent activity rhythm of the littoral fish *Blennius* endures for only about 4 days in CC; when the animals became arrhythmic, Gibson (1967) subjected them to LD 6:6 (60 ft-c) for 6–7 days and found that the fish responded to it by increased activity during the light period. This "rhythm," however, would not then persist in CC.

Organisms with clearly defined solar-day and tidal components in a single function offer additional experimental possibilities, for their circadian component would be expected to respond in the usual way to

LD   cycles. This has been demonstrated to be true, with the following concomitant alteration of the tidal component.

The color-change rhythm of the fiddler crab, *U. pugnax*, is a composite of daily and tidal components. To test the role of LD cycles on these components, fresh crabs were placed in DD and one-half of the group given light between 2400 and 0600 h (150 ft-c) for 3 days. The phase of the diurnal component of the latter was delayed by about 4.9 h and the tidal component by about 4.6 h (Brown, Fingerman, Sandeen, and Webb, 1953). The number of repeated LD cycles needed to bring about a phase change was later found to be a function of the light intensity (Brown, Fingerman, and Hines, 1954).

Using an identical experimental design Bennett and Brown (1959) studied the role of light in shifting the dual components of the activity rhythm of *U. pugnax*. They found that a 3-day exposure between 2400 and 0600 h (100 ft-c) produced a 5.6-h phase shift in the daily component and a 4.4-h shift in the tidal component.

A different design was used with the same species by Webb and Brown (1965). They maintained their crabs in LL (1 ft-c) and added a 2-h interval of brighter light (55 ft-c) in one experiment—and a 4-h pulse in a second experiment—at 24.75-h intervals. This means that the bright light supplement was begun 45 min later each day. They found that the 4-h addition (but not the 2-h one) stretched the interval between tidal peaks to 12.75 h (i.e., the bimodal lunar-day activity rhythm became 25.5 h in length). These authors conclude that the simplest explanation for the 25.5-h period is that the diurnal rhythm was shifted by 45 min each time the light supplement was offered and that this then shifted the tidal rhythm by the same amount. Thus, the 24-h 50-min tidal rhythm, plus the daily 45-min increment, became 25.5 h.

SUMMARY AND CONCLUSIONS

1. The tidal cycle on the home shoreline sets the phase of the inhabitant's rhythms. Even location of a crab burrow on the beach incline plays a determining role.
2. Paradoxically, the periodic wetting of inundation is not an important phase-setting factor for most intertidal organisms. Instead, the effective portions of the tidal cycle are one, or a combination, of the following: (a) First is mechanical agitation, especially for animals living in an uprush zone, where they are periodically subjected to the pounding surf. (b) While they have not yet been systematically investigated, temperature cycles have very pronounced entraining roles in crabs. Intuitively, the author would expect temperature to be a most important phase-setter; but the validity of this supposition must await further observations. (c) Observations thus far suggest

that pressure is probably not a particularly important entraining agent for most intertidal organisms, although it is a very important entraining agent in the life of the green crab.

3. LD cycles in general, whether daily or tidal in length, have no effect on the entrainment or phase-setting of many tidal rhythms. There are two exceptions: (a) A 24-h LD cycle is known to keep a tidal locomotor rhythm (one that becomes circatidal in CC) at a strict tidal frequency. (b) In organismic processes with both daily and tidal components, when the former is shifted by light stimuli, the latter is affected in a nearly identical manner.

Literature Cited

Altevogt, R. 1959. Okologische und ethologische Studien an Europas einziger Winkerkrabb *Uca tangeri*. *Z. Morph. Okol. Tiere*, 48:123–146.

Barnwell, F. H. 1966. Daily and tidal patterns of activity in individual fiddler crabs (Genus *Uca*) from the Woods Hole region. *Biol. Bull.*, 130:1–17.

Barnwell, F. H. 1968. The role of rhythmic systems in the adaptation of fiddler crabs to the intertidal zone. *Amer. Zool.*, 8:569–583.

Barnwell, F. H., and F. A. Brown, Jr. 1963. Differences in the persistent metabolic rhythms of fiddler crabs from two levels of the same beach. *Biol. Bull.*, 125:371.

Bennett, M. F., and F. A. Brown, Jr. 1959. Experimental modification of the lunar rhythm of running activity of the fiddler crab, *Uca pugnax*. *Biol. Bull.*, 117:404.

Brown, F. A., Jr., M. Fingerman, and M. N. Hines. 1954. A study of the mechanism involved in shifting of the phases of the endogenous daily rhythm by light stimuli. *Biol. Bull.*, 106:308–317.

Brown, F. A., Jr., M. Fingerman, M. Sandeen, and H. M. Webb. 1953. Persistent diurnal and tidal rhythms of color change in the fiddler crab, *Uca pugnax*. *J. Exp. Zool.*, 123:29–60.

Brown, F. A., Jr., M. I. Sandeen, and M. Fingerman. 1952. Modifications of the tidal rhythm of *Uca* by tidal differences and by illumination. *Biol. Bull.*, 103:297.

Enright, J. T. 1962. Responses of an amphipod to pressure changes. *Comp Biochem. Physiol.*, 7:131–145.

Enright, J. T. 1963. The tidal rhythm of activity of a sand-beach amphipod. *Z. vergl. Physiol.*, 46:276–313.

Enright, J. T. 1965. Entrainment of a tidal rhythm. *Science*, 147:864–867.

Fingerman, M. 1956. Phase difference in the tidal rhythms of color change of two species of fiddler crabs. *Biol. Bull.*, 110:274–290.

Fingerman, M. 1957. Relation between position of burrows and tidal rhythm of *Uca. Biol. Bull.*, 112:7–20.

Fingerman, M., M. E. Lowe, and W. C. Mobberly, Jr. 1958. Environmental factors involved in setting the phases of the tidal rhythm of color change in the fiddler crabs *Uca pugilator* and *Uca minax. Limnol. Oceanogr.*, 3:271–282.

Gibson, R. N. 1967. Experiments on the tidal rhythm of *Blennius pholis. J. mar. biol. Ass. U. K.*, 47:97–111.

Gibson, R. N. 1971. Factors affecting the rhythmic activity of *Blennius pholis* L. (Teleostei). *Anim. Behav.*, 19:336–343.

Hastings, J. W. 1964. The role of light in persistent daily rhythms. In A. Giese, Ed., *Photophysiology*, Vol. I. Academic, New York.

Hopkins, J. T. 1966. The role of water in the behaviour of an estuarine mud-flat diatom. *J. mar. biol. Ass. U. K.*, 46:617–626.

Jones, D. A., and E. Naylor. 1970. The swimming rhythm of the sand beach isopod *Eurydice pulchra. J. exp. mar. Biol. Ecol.*, 4:188–199.

Klapow, L. A. 1972. Natural and artificial rephasing of a tidal rhythm. *J. Comp. Physiol.*, 79:233–258.

Morgan, E. 1965. The activity rhythm of the amphipod *Corophium volutator* (Pallas) and its possible relationship to changes in hydrostatic pressure associated with the tides. *J. Anim. Ecol.*, 34:731–746.

Morgan, E. 1973. On the pressure response of *Eurydice* (Isopoda). Mar. *Behav. Physiol.*, 1:323–339.

Morgan, E., A. Nelson-Smith, and E. W. Knight-Jones. 1964. Responses of *Nymphon gracile* to pressure cycles of tidal frequency. *J. Exp. Biol.*, 41:825–836.

Naylor, E. 1960. Locomotory rhythms in *Carcinus maenas* (L) from nontidal conditions. *J. Exp. Biol.*, 37:482–488.

Naylor, E., and R. J. Atkinson. 1972. Pressure and the rhythmic behaviour of inshore marine animals. In M. Sleigh and G. Alister, Eds., *The Effects of pressure on organisms*. Academic, New York, pp. 395–415.

Naylor, E., R. J. Atkinson, and B. Williams. 1971. External factors influencing the tidal rhythm of shore crabs. *J. interdiscipl. Cycle Res.*, 2:173–180.

Palmer, J. D. 1960. The role of moisture and illumination on the expression of the rhythmic behavior of the diatom, *Hantzschia amphioxys. Biol. Bull.*, 119:330.

Palmer, J. D., and F. E. Round. 1967. Persistent, vertical-migration rhythms in benthic microflora. VI. The tidal and diurnal nature of the rhythm in the diatom *Hantzschia virgata. Biol. Bull.*, 132:44–55.

Rodriguez, G., and E. Naylor. 1972. Behavioural rhythms in littoral prawns. *J. mar. biol. Ass. U. K.,* 52:81–95.

Webb, H. M. 1966. Pigmentary rhythms as indicators of neurosecretion. *Amer. Zool.,* 6:181–186.

Webb, H. M. 1971. Effects of artificial 24-hour cycles on the tidal rhythm of activity in the fiddler crab, *Uca pugnax. J. interdiscipl. Cycle Res.,* 2:191–198.

Webb, H. M. 1972. Phasing of locomotor activity in the fiddler crab, *Uca pugnax. J. interdiscipl. Cycle Res.,* 3:179–185.

Webb, H. M., and F. A. Brown, Jr. 1965. Interactions of diurnal and tidal rhythms in the fiddler crab, *Uca pugnax. Biol. Bull.,* 129:582–591.

Wilkins, M. B. 1960. The effect of light upon plant rhythms. *Cold Spring Harbor Symp. Quant. Biol.,* 25:115–129.

Williams, B. G., and E. Naylor. 1969. Synchronization of the locomotor tidal rhythm of *Carcinus. J. Exp. Biol.,* 51:715–725.

8 Temperature

INTRODUCTION

Among some of the more fascinating aspects of biological rhythms is the influence of temperature on the period and phase (see Sweeney and Hastings, 1960, and Wilkins, 1965, for a general review of effect of temperature on circadian rhythms). Property-revealing experiments on circadian rhythms fall into three categories: *step* experiments where the constant ambient temperature of an experimental setup is abruptly raised or lowered and then held constant at this new level; *single pulse* experiments, in which a temperature is raised or lowered for a relatively short interval; and *cyclic pulse* treatments, which were discussed in the preceding chapter under "Temperature Entrainment." The changes produced by these separate procedures are quite different.

The rationale behind the step approach is this: Underlying and governing tidal rhythms is thought to be a "living" horologe whose components are of necessity physiochemical. Temperature is known to affect profoundly the rate at which simple chemical reactions proceed and, less greatly, but distinctly, physical processes. So, by changing an organism's body temperature, and therefore that of its clock, the rate at which the latter runs should be altered (if the clockworks are simple), and this change will be signaled to the observer as a similar alteration in the period of the organism's overt rhythm. Philosophically, however, all clocks—grandfather, cesium, or living—would cease to be timepieces if the rate at which they ran were altered by the vagaries of enviromental temperature changes.

Experimentation on circadian rhythms has demonstrated that little change in period is produced with stepwise increases or decreases in temperature (Figure 3-2). For example, the average temperature coefficient of 25 separate studies culled from the literature is 1.1, rather than a value somewhere between 2 and 5, which would be expected if the horologe was a simple biochemical mechanism.

Circadian rhythms subjected to single pulses of temperature are usually rephased: the peaks being either advanced or delayed in relation to controls. The direction and magnitude of the change produced are functions of three parameters of the pulse: the size of the temperature change it provides, its duration, and the time in the circadian cycle it is offered. To expand on the latter, it has been found that underlying an organism's response to temperature pulses is a rhythm in the organism's sensitivity to the pulse. For example, pulses identical in temperature change and duration differ in magnitude and direction of phase change that they produce, simply as a function of time of day that they are offered to an organism (Figure 8-1). Although this aspect of pulse response has not yet been worked out in a great number of organisms [Bünning (1967) provides a good summary], the form of this rhythm appears to be fairly similar from one organism to the next. This changing sensitivity pattern is here referred to as the *temperature phase-setting rhythm.*

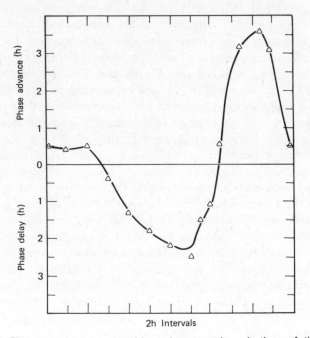

Figure 8-1. The temperature sensitive phase-setting rhythm of the eclosion rhythm of *Drosophila pseudoobscura*. The fruit fly undergoes a persistent daily rhythm in the emergence of adults from their puparia in DD. This figure shows the phase advances and delays produced in the eclosion rhythm by subjecting the pupae to 12-h low-temperature pulses (28° to 20° and then back up to 28°) begun at the times indicated on the abscissa. Clearly the magnitude and direction of phase changes are a function of the time at which the low pulses are given (modified from Zimmerman, Pittendrigh, and Pavlidis, 1968).

The role of temperature in manipulating tidal rhythms has not yet been studied in a systematic fashion. Many of the studies reported in the literature represent, at most, pilot projects, but follow-up work never seems to be forthcoming. The rationale for undertaking much of the work that is done is never stated nor are the ecological or horological implications of the results. As a result, there is a dearth of knowledge on the role of temperature—including cyclic pulsing—on tidal rhythms. Certainly this aspect is worthy of considerable future work. We do not know, for example, whether as general properties the period of tidal rhythms are actually temperature-independent, whether the tidal clock can be truly stopped or uncoupled from its overt rhythm, or whether a temperature phase-response curve underlies tidal rhythms. A summary of our very fragmentary knowledge follows.

TEMPERATURE "INDEPENDENCE" OF THE PERIOD

The color-change rhythm in the fiddler crab, U. pugnax, is predominately a daily one but has superimposed on it a tidal modulating component (Chapter 4). The daily component was shown to be temperature-independent between 6° and 26°C (Brown and Webb, 1948). This was verified by Stephens (1955). Because of the low amplitude and complicated efforts required to extract the tidal component, its susceptibility to temperature was not deemed practical for study at the time. A means was later found.

Hines (1953, 1954) discovered that the degree of concentration of pigment in the crab's legs, 30 min after induced autotomy, mimicked the tidal ebb and flow on the crab's home beach. She noted that during the subjective day—when the leg pigments were maximally dispersed [in crabs maintained in LL (dim)]—if legs were removed during the times corresponding to low tides, little pigment concentration occurred. But, if the legs were removed during high tide a significant concentration of pigment took place within the span of a half hour.

This facet of color change was then used by Brown, Webb, Bennett, and Sandeen (1954) to study the effect of different constant temperatures on the tidal rhythm. Prior to and during induced autotomy, the crabs were placed in temperatures of 13°, 22.5°, and 30°C. Subsequent observations over the next few hours of pigment movements in isolated legs showed that the tidal rhythm persisted unchanged throughout the 17° temperature range, suggesting, of course, that the period of the tidal component of the color-change rhythms was also temperature-independent.

The temperature-independent nature of the tidal locomotory rhythm in the green crab, C. maenas, was elucidated by Naylor (1963). Freshly collected "shore crabs" were placed into LL (dim) and constant temperatures of 10°, 15°, 20°, and 25°C for 3 days. During this time there was no indication of a lengthening or shortening of the period of the crab's rhythm (Figure 8-2). The same is true of the circadian rhythm in

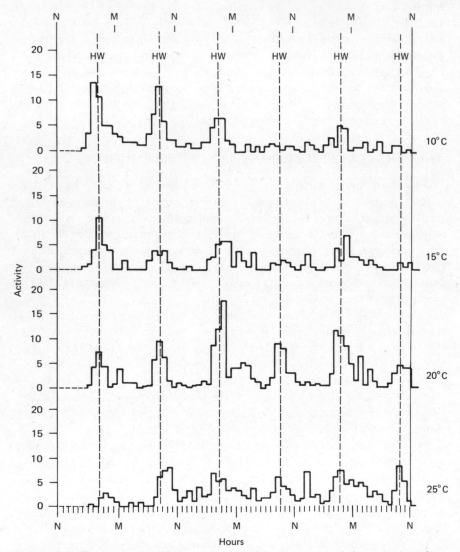

Figure 8-2. The average activity patterns of four groups of three crabs (*Carcinus maenas*) transferred from 15°C to the test temperatures indicated and LL (dim). HW represents the midpoints of high tides in nature (Naylor, 1963).

"dock crabs" maintained in constant temperatures between 15° and 26°C (Naylor, 1960).

Even though the period is temperature-independent, just after the introduction of a temperature step a temporary phase change of the first activity peak is produced. A temperature increase causes a phase delay and a temperature stepdown produces an advance, the magnitude of the alteration (which never exceeds ±3 h) varies directly with the size of the temperature step (Figure 8-3). The response is a temporary one, and the second peak after the step is back in phase with controls (Naylor, Atkinson, and Williams, 1971).

Morgan (1965) reports that the amphipod (*Corophium*) locomotor rhythm is temperature-independent between 5° and 25°C; but he ob-

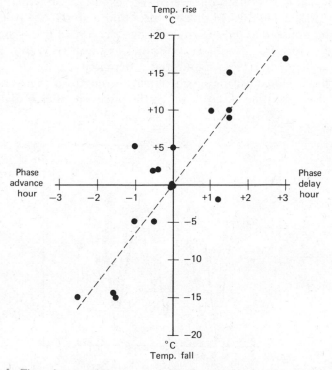

Figure 8-3. The phase advance or delay expressed by the first peak of the activity rhythm after transfer of green crab, *Carcinus maenas,* to either lower or higher (respectively) temperatures. Zero temperature on the ordinate represents a starting temperature close to 15°C. The phase alterations are temporary ones, the second peak after the temperature step being back in phase with controls (Naylor, Atkinson, and Williams, 1971).

served the animals in these temperatures for only 1½ cycles, and from his figure there appears to be a slight lengthening of the period at lower temperatures.

Rao (1954) reports temperature-independence of the filtering rhythm in the mussel, *Mytilus*. He held the clams at temperatures of 9°, 14°, and 20°C for 4 weeks and observed no change at all in the period length.

TEMPERATURE PULSE STIMULI

A plethora of temperature pulse experiments (more in fact and with more purpose in mind) have been performed on the fiddler crab, *Uca*, than on any other intertidal animal. Unfortunately, these experiments were restricted only to the animal's circadian rhythms because the tidal component had not yet been discovered. For example, Brown and Webb, as early as 1948, demonstrated that a 6-h cold pulse (0°–3°C) given during the morning hours, delayed the color-change rhythm by 6 h—apparently stopping the clock for that interval of time (Figure 8-4). Webb, Bennett. Graves, and Stephens (1953) found that a 6-h exposure to 5°C also produced a phase change but never one equal in length to the duration of the cold pulse. The time of day at which the pulse was offered determined

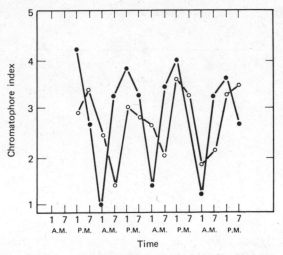

Figure 8-4. The result of a 6-h immersion in 0–3°C seawater on the color-change rhythm of the fiddler crab, *Uca pugnax*. Open circles represent control populations of five animals; solid circles represent the average responses of five cold-treated crabs now in DD and 16°C (modified from Brown and Webb, 1948).

the degree of inhibition of the amplitude of the rhythm. Apparently a 5°C pulse does not stop the clock (as does a 0°–3°C pulse) but functions instead to change the setting of the clock's "hands."

Stephens (1957), using a less harsh treatment, found that temperature pulses of 18°–9.5°–18°C given for a duration of between 6 and 12 h caused phase delays in the fiddler crab color-change rhythm of between 1.5 and 5 h depending on the time of day at which the pulses were begun. After treatment, the new phase lasted for at least 10 days. The magnitude of the phase changes that are produced are apparently the expression of an underlying bimodal temperature-sensitivity rhythm, with peaks occurring in the early morning and afternoon (Figure 8-5).

Single temperature pulses also bring about interesting changes in the green crab activity rhythm (Naylor, 1963). Exposing crabs previously maintained at 15° to 4.0°, 5.5°, or 10.0°C for several hours inhibited all activity during the low temperatures. On return to 15°C, those that had been exposed to 10° resumed their rhythms in phase with control crabs—apparently their tidal clocks had continued to run throughout the low-temperature treatment in spite of the fact that their overt rhythm was not expressed (Figure 8-6A). Those exposed to experimental temperatures of 4.0° or 5.5°C for at least 6 h were found to be phase-shifted by the treatment: immediately on rewarming to 15°C a burst of activity occurred and was followed by subsequent peaks spaced at 12.4-h intervals (Figure 8-6B and D). The new phase would persist for 5 days in CC. [An identical response has been described for the isopod *Eurydice* (Jones

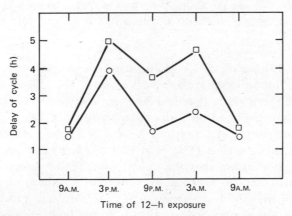

Figure 8-5. The phase delays caused by a 12-h cold pulse (18°–9.5°–18°), beginning at the times corresponding with the points. The changes produced are in the fiddler crab (*Uca pugnax*) color-change rhythm (modified from Stephens, 1957).

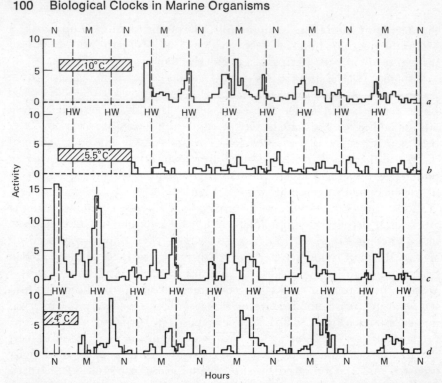

Figure 8-6. The effect of low-temperature pulses on the phase of the tidal rhythm in *Carcinus maenus*. A 24-h 10°C sojourn has no effect on the phase of the rhythm (A), but exposure to 5.5°C for the same length of time causes a rephase (B), as does an 11-h cold pulse of 4°C (compare C with D). HW represents midpoints of high tide in nature (modified from Naylor, 1963).

and Naylor, 1970) with a 3-h temperature pulse (15°–5°–15°C)]. This property was used to explore another aspect of the green crab rhythms.

C. maenus shore crabs that had become arrhythmic in captivity and dock crabs that displayed only circadian rhythms in CC could be made to display persistent tidal rhythms by exposing them for 8 h to 4°C (Figure 8-7). On return to 15°C (and LL) the first tidal peaks appeared immediately (indicating that the "pulse" was really acting like a step), and subsequent ones followed at tidal intervals. [Identical results were obtained with arrhythmic *Nassarius* (Stephens, Sandeen, and Webb, 1953) and *Eurydice* (Jones and Naylor, 1970)]. It was later found that the entire crab need not be chilled to induce the rhythm. In an ingenious experiment, a tether was devised that immobilized a crab in a 15°C constant temperature bath, while 1°C iced seawater was dripped onto its

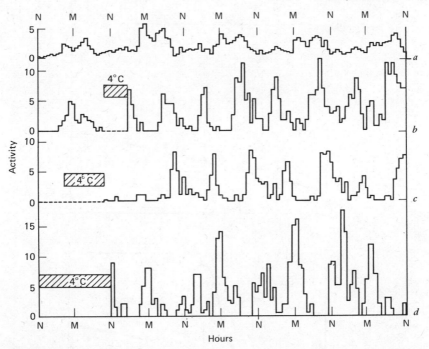

Figure 8-7. The effect of cold pulses in initiating the tidal component in *Carcinus maenas* activity. *A*, nocturnal rhythm in crabs collected from a non-tidal habitat; *B, C, D*, initiation of a tidal rhythm in these crabs by 8, 13, and 24-h, 4°C-temperature pulses (Naylor, 1963).

exposed eyestalks for 10–11 h. This treatment proved to be as effective as was the "Chinese water torture" after which it was patterned, in that activity was obediently molded into a tidal rhythm as effectively as whole-body chilling (Figure 8-8). Again, the X-organ/sinus-gland complex is implicated (Naylor and Williams, 1968).

Enright (1963) performed some pilot temperature-pulse experiments on the amphipod (*Synchilidium*) activity rhythm. In one brief series he dropped the ambient temperature from 20° to 10°C for 24 h and, after raising it again to the starting point, found a delay of the following peaks of about three-quarters of an hour. In another series, he pulsed upward for 2 h from 15° to 28°C and found that if the pulse was offered during their active phase it produced a 1-h delay in the following peak, but when it was offered during times of quiescence, it had no effect. The latter suggests the existence of an underlying rhythm in sensitivity to temperature.

When the littoral fish, *Blennius,* is maintained in the laboratory for

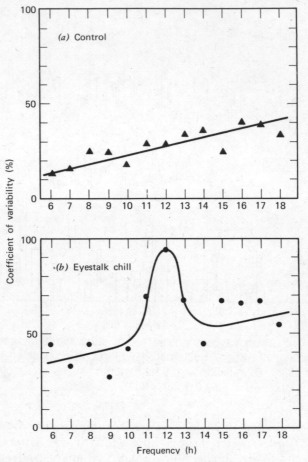

Figure 8-8. Induction of tidal rhythm in arrhythmic green crabs (*Carcinus maenas*). (*A*) Unchilled control animals. (*B*) Periodogram analysis of three arrhythmic crabs whose eyestalks were chilled to 1°C for ~10 h; a tidal period was created (Naylor and Williams, 1968).

several weeks, it becomes arrhythmic. Gibson (1967) reported that following a 4-h exposure to 10°C, a tidal rhythm is reinitiated. However, in a subsequent study (1971), he found that chilling down to 3°C for 12 h had no effffect.

Fincham (1970) has reported that a 6-h cold pulse (10°–1°–10°C) produced a 3-h delay in the *Bathyporeia* activity rhythm. His limited data suggest that a temperature-sensitivity rhythm might well underlie this response.

SUMMARY AND CONCLUSIONS

1. The role of temperature on tidal rhythms is compared with its role on circadian rhythms.
2. The effect of different constant temperatures has been studied on only four tidal rhythms thus far. In each case no permanent change in period was found, which is not the case with most circadian rhythms, the latter having temperature coefficients around 1.1. In two of the studies, the rhythms under test temperatures were followed for less than a day, and a third study (as mentioned in Chapter 6) cannot be repeated. Certainly much work remains to be done.
3. Short exposure to very cold temperature pulses produces a response that may be interpreted as a temporary stoppage of the clock. Exposure to relatively less cold pulses appeared simply to reset the hands of the clock. The same responses have been demonstrated with circadian rhythms.
4. In the case of green crabs that had become arrhythmic during prolonged captivity in the laboratory, a tidal rhythm could be reinitiated by a single short cold treatment. The cold pulse also set the phase of the rhythm.
5. A few superficial studies employing temperature steps or pulses have produced results that suggest that a phase-change sensitivity rhythm—just as found associated with circadian rhythms—may underlie tidal rhythms. Certainly a determined search for this rhythm should be made in the near future.

Literature Cited

Brown, F. A., Jr., and H. M. Webb. 1948. Temperature relations of an endogenous daily rhythmicity in the fiddler crab, *Uca. Physiol. Zool.,* 21:371–381.

Brown, F. A., Jr., H. M. Webb, M. F. Bennett, and M. I. Sandeen. 1954. Temperature-independence of the frequency of the endogenous tidal rhythm of *Uca. Physiol. Zool,.* 27:345–349.

Bünning, E. 1973. *The Physiological Clock.* Springer-Verlag, New York.

Enright, J. T. 1963. The tidal rhythm of activity of a sand-beach amphipod. *Z. vergl. Physiol.,* 46:276–313.

Fincham, A. A. 1970. Rhythmic behaviour of the intertidal amphipod *Bathyporeia pelagica. J. mar. biol. Ass. U. K.,* 50:1057–1068.

Gibson, R. N. 1967. Experiments on the tidal rhythm of *Blennius pholis. J. mar. biol. Ass. U. K.,* 47:97–111.

Gibson, R. N. 1971. Factors affecting the rhythmic activity of *Blennius pholis* L. (Teleostei). *Anim. Behav.,* 19:336–343.

Hines, M. N. 1953. Use of autotomized legs in determining the phases of the tidal rhythm in *Uca pugnax. Biol. Bull.,* 105:375–376.

Hines, M. N. 1954. A tidal rhythm in behavior of melanophores in auto-tomized legs of *Uca pugnax*. *Biol. Bull.*, 107:386–396.

Jones, D. A., and E. Naylor. 1970. The swimming rhythm of the sand beach isopod *Eurydice pulchra*. *J. exp. mar. Biol. Ecol.*, 4:188–199.

Morgan, E. 1965. The activity rhythm of the amphipod *Corophium volutator* (Pallas) and its possible relationship to changes in hydro-static pressure associated with the tides. *J. Anim. Ecol.*, 34:731–746.

Naylor, E. 1960. Locomotory rhythms in *Carcinus maenas* (L) from non-tidal conditions. *J. Exp. Biol.*, 37:482–488.

Naylor, E. 1963. Temperature relationships of the locomotor rhythm of *Carcinus*. *J. Exp. Biol.*, 40:669–679.

Naylor, E., R. Atkinson, and B. Williams. 1971. External factors influ-encing the tidal rhythm of shore crabs. *J. interdiscipl. Cycle Res.*, 2:173–180.

Naylor, E., and B. Williams. 1968. Effects of eyestalk removal on rhythmic locomotor activity in *Carcinus*. *J. Exp. Biol.*, 49:107–116.

Rao, K. P. 1954. Tidal rhythmicity of rate of water propulsion in *Mytilus*, and its modifiability by transplantation. *Biol. Bull.*, 106:353–359.

Stephens, G. C. 1955. Responses of the diurnal melanophore rhythm of *Uca pugnax* to changes in temperature. *Biol. Bull.*, 109:352.

Stephens, G. C. 1957. Influence of temperature fluctuations on the diurnal melanophore rhythm of the fiddler crab, *Uca*. *Physiol. Zool.*, 30:55–69.

Stephens, G. C., M. I. Sandeen, and H. M. Webb. 1953. A persistent tidal rhythm of activity in the mud snail, *Nassa obsoleta*. *Anat. Rec.*, 117:635.

Sweeney, B. M., and J. W. Hastings. 1960. Effects of temperature upon diurnal rhythms. *Cold Spring Harbor Symp. Quant. Biol.*, 25:87–104.

Webb, H. M., M. F. Bennett, R. C. Graves, and G. C. Stephens. 1953. Relationship between time of day and inhibiting influence of low temperature on the diurnal chromatophore rhythm of *Uca*. *Biol. Bull.*, 105:386–387.

Wilkins, M. B. 1965. The influence of temperature and temperature changes on biological clocks. In J. Aschoff, Ed. *Circadian Clocks* North-Holland Publ. Co., Amsterdam, pp. 146–163.

Zimmerman, W. F., C. S. Pittendrigh, and T. Pavlidis. 1968. Tempera-ture compensation of the circadian oscillation in *Drosophila pseudo-obscura* and its entrainment by temperature cycles. *J. Insect Physiol.*, 14:669–684.

9 A Potpourri of Lunar Related Rhythms

Up to this point, we essentially have limited our discussion to rhythms displaying two peaks per lunar day. Three other categories will now be considered: unimodal lunar-day, fortnightly, and monthly rhythms.

UNIMODAL LUNAR-DAY CLOCK-ASSOCIATED RESPONSES

A beach-dwelling amphipod, *Talitrus saltator*, lives in the wet sand of the supralittoral zone just above the breaking waves. During the morning and early afternoon the animals remain buried in subterranean refuges but venture forth in the late afternoon and at nighttime. The cool humidity during the hours of darkness lowers the risk of desiccation and the "sand-hoppers" may wander inland as far as 100 m. They return to their seaside habitat in the early morning. To perform these migrations, the tiny animals employ both solar-day and lunar-day clocks and use the sun (or the vibrational plane of polarized skylight) and the moon to orient themselves during their wanderings.

To quantify their movements, a sample population was placed in a large concave glass vessel surrounded by a curtain that screened out all potential landmarks below the horizon but permitted a full view of the heavens. The glass vessel was divided into 16 walled sectors, and the position of the animals in the container was determined by time-lapse photography through the bottom.

Animals were captured at the inland terminus of their journeys and sealed hermetically in the orientation apparatus in dry air (the dryness providing the stimulus necessary to initiate "escape" movements). On moonlit nights the animals were found to accumulate on the seaward margin of the container (Figure 9-1), but on moonless nights they distributed themselves randomly throughout the chamber (Papi, 1960: Enright, 1972b).

To demonstrate that it truly was the moon being used as a heavenly signpost, the animals in the training vessel were prevented from seeing

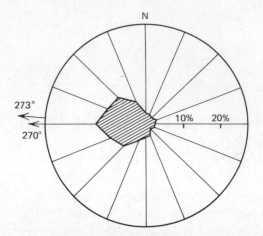

Figure 9-1. The moon orientation displayed by the amphipod *Talitrus saltator*. The escape direction (i.e., the route back to the shoreline) was 270° due west; the recorded orientation of 3108 individuals in the observation apparatus was 273° (modified from Papi and Pardi, 1959).

the full moon at its normal position in the sky by an opaque screen. The treatment caused them to become disoriented. When the moon's image was then presented to them as a reflection in a mirror (Figure 9-2)—that is, shining in from a new azimuth to one side of the screen—or when a flashlight was used to simulate the face of the full moon, the escape direction was altered appropriately so that the angle assumed with the artificial moon was essentially identical to the one previously adopted with the real moon.

The moon, of course, is not a stationary reference point, for it moves from east, through south, to west across the night sky. Therefore, to maintain the proper escape direction, the amphipods must continually change their orientation angle with the moon. During most all-night studies, they do this, but for as yet unexplained reasons, on occasional nights they do not (Papi, 1960). Enright (1972b) has found the same relationship to hold for another talitrid, *Orchestoidea corniculata* (Figure 9-3). To produce the proper orientational change, these organisms must have a clock signaling the hours of the lunar-day (Papi, 1960). Or, saying it another way, only by knowing the time of the lunar day and the angle to assume at each instant can the proper angle back to the beach be guaranteed.

By collecting the amphipods 1–14 days before the night of testing and storing them in DD, it was demonstrated that the lunar-day clock con-

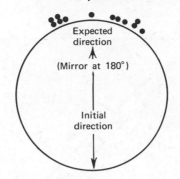

Figure 9-2. The effect of an illusory change in position of the moon in the sky by reflecting its image in a mirror from a different direction. When the talitrids were permitted to see the moon, they accumulated on the side of the chamber indicated by the initial-direction arrow. When the moon was screened from view and the image reflected from an angle 180° from normal, the animals still approximated the previous angle (signified by the arrow labeled "expected direction") with the reflection. Each point outside the circle represents the mean path of separate experiments (modified from Enright, 1972).

tinued to run without periodic exposure to the moon (Papi, 1960; Enright, 1972b). The amphipods tested correctly after this treatment. This is a somewhat unexpected response, for, as we have seen before, the lunar-day period underlying the response would be expected to assume a circa frequency in CC. While this change was not apparent in the average escape route chosen by the test population, it might have occurred at the level of the individual, for the scatter around the mean response increased with time in DD. This variability would be expected if some animals' periods were lengthened while others were shortened. An effect similar to this has been described by Stephens (1962) for fiddler crab color-change rhythms and by Lowe, Hinds, Lardner, and Justice (1967) for kangaroo rat and Gila monster activity rhythms.

During the early morning and the late afternoon, talitrids use the sun as their reference point, and compensate for its movement via the use of their solar-day clock. A particular escape direction is a characteristic of a local population; for example a population living on the north shore of a large bay will have a due south direction of escape, while others dwelling on the south shore of the same bay will escape to the north. The direction is quite ingrained in the animals, as was demonstrated by transporting a sample from the west coast of Italy (where the escape route back to the sea was westerly) overland to the Adriatic side of the country (where the escape direction should be to the east). When

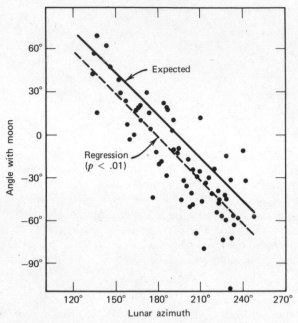

Figure 9-3. The changing orientation angle assumed by the sandhopper *Orchestoidea corniculata* as the moon moved across the night sky. The figure includes data from six different nights of experimentation. The correct escape direction (i.e., a path perpendicular to the home shoreline) was at azimuth 193°. Each point is the average path of about 20 amphipods (modified from Enright, 1972).

the orientational preference was tested at the new location, the animals chose west—the direction of safety on their home beaches (Papi, 1960). In an identical experiment involving a greater translocation distance, a population was shipped from Italy to Argentina, and was tested there after 14 days in DD. The results showed that the animals' clocks were still running on Italian time (Papi, 1955).

In fact, the escape route of individual populations has been found to be determined genetically. This was demonstrated by collecting animals from distinct populations, each of which displayed its own escape direction (Figure 9-4A), and allowing them to reproduce in the laboratory. The offspring, which had never seen the sun nor its progression across the sky, were subsequently taken into the field and their orientation tested. All chose the direction used by their parents before them (Figure 9-4B) (Pardi, 1960).

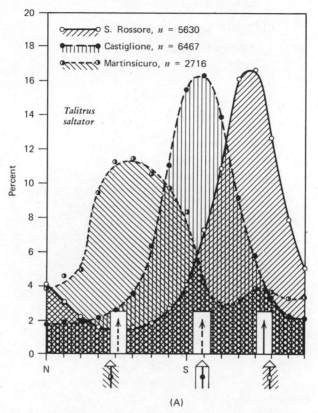

(A)

Figure 9-4. Proof of the genetic basis of the escape direction in separate populations of beach hoppers (*Talitrus saltator*). (A) Frequency distributions of escape routes taken by three parent populations. The vertical bold arrows indicate the correct directions; the light arrows arising from the abscissa indicate the average observed paths.

FORTNIGHTLY RHYTHMS

As described in the first chapter, the gravitational fields of the sun and moon summate twice each month to produce the spring tides (Figure 1-8). Synchronized with these fortnightly (14.7-day) changes in tidal amplitude are a variety of organismic displays—usually fortnightly breeding cycles.

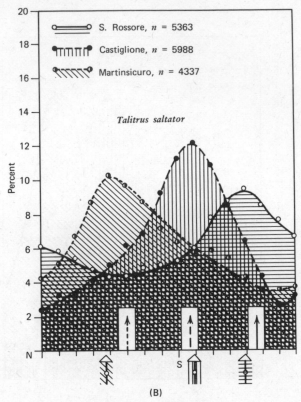

(B) Frequency distributions of offspring of the parent populations described above (symbols the same). These individuals were bred in captivity and had never seen the sun or sky before testing (modified from Pardi, 1960).

Algae

Observations in the field have disclosed that many marine algae liberate their reproductive products on a periodic basis, usually twice a month. The brown alga *Dictyota dichotoma* is an example of such a plant. In late summer, sperm and eggs are liberated at fortnightly intervals (14–15 days apart), each release being completed in just a few hours (Williams, 1905; Hoyt, 1907, 1927). Since fertilization is left mostly to chance encounters between egg and sperm, the periodicity is of obvious value, for it greatly enhances the probability of gamete union.

When Müller (1962) cultured *Dictyota* under natural day–night cycles and counted the number of eggs released, he found that the 15-day rhythm persisted. But when he subjected his cultures to LD 14:10 in the lab, the rhythm was not displayed. Feeling that moonlight was the missing stimulus in the artificial conditions of the laboratory, he left the over-head lights on for one night (his idea of simulating the full moon). Ten days later a small burst of eggs was released, and this event repeated with greater amplitude at about 17-day intervals for the next 2½ months (Figure 9-5). Vielhaben (1963) confirmed these findings.

Hollenberg, working back in 1936, reported that the green alga *Halicystis ovalis* (the gametophyte stage of *Derbesia*) formed gametangia only during spring tides and that this periodicity would persist in the lab in the absence of the tide. More recently, Page and Sweeney (1968) studied reproduction in the closely related species *H. parvula* (the game-tophyte stage of *Derbesia tenuissima*) and found no persistent fortnightly rhythm.

Invertebrates

Gross observations in the field of the little flatworm, *Convoluta rosco-fensis* (Chapter 3), revealed that the colonies appeared to undergo a fort-nightly alteration in size, being most extensive just before the spring

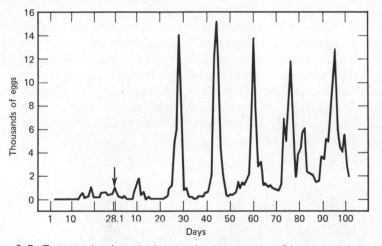

Figure 9-5. Egg-production rhythm in the brown alga *Dictyota dichotoma*, in LD 14:10 and 20°C. One dark period, indicated by the falling arrow, was omitted—the artificial light applied during this time representing the full moon. This single treatment initiated a rhythm that displayed a period of about 17 days (modified from Müller, 1962).

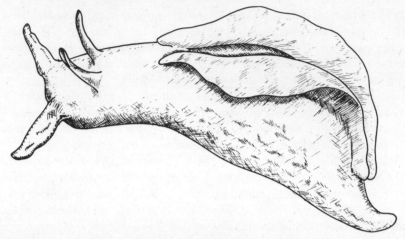

Figure 9-6. The sea hare, *Aplysia californica.*

tides. However, microscopic examination of individuals disclosed that at the onset of spring tides, the animals begin to discharge their eggs, and in *Convoluta,* this is rather self-destructive: during the process the posterior end of the animal is jetisoned and remains buried in the sand. Only the anterior portion continues the vertical migration rhythm to the surface, giving the impression to a casual observer that the colony has been reduced in numbers by one-half (Keeble, 1910).

Within the abdominal ganglion of the sea hare, *Aplysia californica,* a snail with a vestigial shell (Figure 9-6), are some very large neuron cell bodies, each of which can be easily located by its size. One of the cells of this ganglion spontaneously and periodically emits a small burst of spikes followed by a period of silence. The interval between individual spikes in a single burst form a parabola when plotted, so that the cell has been named "the parabolic burster." Its spontaneous activity over a short period of time looks like this:

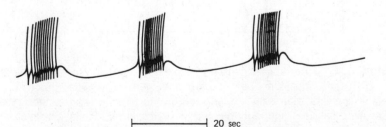

|——————————| 20 sec

If the entire abdominal ganglion is removed from the sea hare, placed in a thermostatically controlled chamber, and perfused with seawater, it will remain healthy for up to 48 h. Here, removed from the peripheral receptors, hormones, and other fluctuating blood-borne compounds, the parabolic-burster cell not only repeats its monotonous short-term routine, but the frequency of the burst output varies in a circadian pattern, with the major peak centered around the time of the previous dark–light transition to which the intact animal had been exposed (Strumwasser, 1965). This rhythm is present even when sea hares are maintained in constant light for up to 10 days before the isolated ganglia are tested. These findings have been confirmed by Lickey, Zack, and Birrell (1971).

Daily sampling of a population of sea hares synchronized to a common LD cycle revealed that a fortnightly rhythm was present in the time of day at which peak spike activity occurred. As seen in Figure 9-7, the daily peaks tended to occur 1.5 h before the time of light-on just after the days of first and third quarters of the moon and fall about the same amount

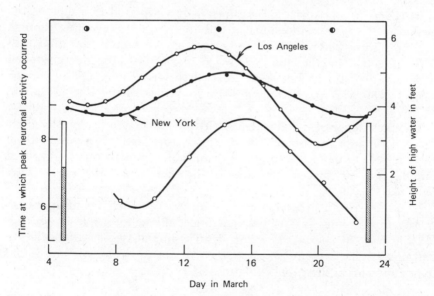

Figure 9-7. Fortnightly rhythm in the time at which the daily maximum of spontaneous spike output occurs in the sea hare parabolic-burster cell. As signified by the vertical bars at each ordinate, light-on occurred just after 7 A.M. Approximately one week after third quarter of the moon (☽) peak spike activity occurred about 1.5 h before the time of light-on; a few days after new moon (●) the daily maximum came about 1.5 h after the light–dark transition. The upper curves represent the fortnightly rhythm in tidal depth at Los Angeles (where the animals were collected) and New York (close to where the study was done in the laboratory) (modified from Strumwasser, 1965).

of time after the dark–light transition soon after new and full moons. The rhythm appears to be in phase with the semimonthly cycle of tidal amplitude on the East Coast, where the experiments were performed (in the laboratory), rather than with the West Coast tides from which the animals were originally collected and shipped.

The above studies are particularly interesting because they show that small isolated segments of multicellular organisms are still capable of maintaining rhythmic behavior.

The isopod, *Excirolana* (Figure 2-18) has been shown to undergo a fortnightly rhythm in molting. Prior to ecdysis, minerals are stored in dermoliths, which are calcium carbonate and phosphate concretions in the fourth and fifth thoracic segments. At molt, the dermoliths dissolve and the salts are used in the recalcification of the new, fully expanded exoskeleton. The actual casting of the skin takes place in two stages: first, the posterior half is shed, and then, about 25 h later, the anterior exoskeleton is cast.

By collecting isopods at 2-day intervals over a period of a month, and measuring the size of individual dermoliths (which are visible through the translucent body wall) and by recording the number of animals in the half-molt stage, the molt cycle was defined. Most animals were found to be molting during one week intervals prior to new and full moon (Figure 9-8), with peaks coming 4–5 days before spring tides (Klapow, 1972).

The persistence of this fortnightly rhythm was tested by transferring a small population of isopods to the laboratory and maintaining them there for 3 months in LL (dim). High mortality had an obscuring effect, but the data do suggest that a weak fortnightly periodicity may have persisted.

E. chiltoni is an ovoviviparous species and gravid females appear to release their young just before new and full moon. At least, animals identified as "newborns" (first larval stage animals with no food in gut and no external symbionts yet attached to the exoskeleton) were found to be abundant at these times (Figure 9-8).

Vertebrates

The grunion, *Leuresthes tenuis*, is a small fish living off the coast of California. In March, April, and May, on the nights just after new and full moon, and at the peaks of spring tides, "runs" consisting of thousands of fish come ashore. As the tide crests, males and females ride the waves up onto the sand beach, where in a writhing courtship out of the water, they mate and deposit their eggs under the sand. The adults return to the sea, until the next spring tide two weeks later. The eggs, meanwhile, develop in the warm sand to a point where, when the wave action of the

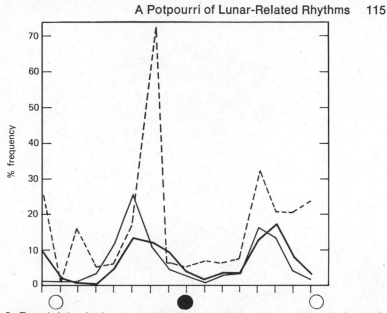

Figure 9-8. Fortnightly rhythm in molting and birth in the sand-beach isopod, *Excirolana chiltoni*. Bold curve represents animals in half-molt condition; the tenuous line represents animals containing full-size dermoliths; and the dashed curve represents "newborn" animals. See text for details. All data represent field observations. Open spheres represent nights of full moon, and the solid one, the new moon (modified from Klapow, 1972).

next high spring tide uncovers them, they hatch and become aquatic (Thompson, 1919; Clark, 1925). It is not known if this behavior is under the partial control of a biological clock, nor has a simple means of investigating this possibility been forthcoming.

SYNODIC MONTHLY RHYTHMS (29.5 Days)

Marine Species

The Pacific Palolo worm (*Eunice viridis*) of Samoa and Fiji and the Atlantic species (*E. fuctata*) both reproduce only during short segments of 2 consecutive months each year. More precisely, reproduction is mainly restricted to usually 1 day in each of these months: the day of (or near) last quarter of the moon (Woodworth, 1903; Burrows, 1945).

The worm lives in the honeycomb tunnels of coral reefs in fairly shallow waters. In preparation for its breeding spree, a string of rudimentary segments are produced by budding from the posterior end of the worm (Figure 9-9). This protrusion, or *epitoke* as it is called, becomes literally engorged with either eggs or sperm, which arise from the peritoneal lining

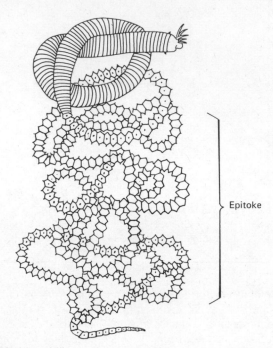

Epitoke

Figure 9-9. *Eunice viridis.*

of the worm's body cavity. As if on a prearranged signal, the foot-long epitokes of many of the members of the reef are broken off at sunrise, and being positively phototactic and negatively geotactic, swim in incredible numbers to the surface waters. Here they writhe, churning up the water, and were it not for their bluish green or reddish brown coloration (egg- and sperm-bearing epitokes, respectively) they would resemble boiling spaghetti. Their gyrations and contractions eventually cause long rents to appear in their bodies, explosively librating their gametes in such numbers that the sea becomes a milky scum.

Each "rising" is a time of celebration for the natives of Somoa and Fiji, and whole villages go to sea to scoop up the worms in cans, washtubs, and aprons. Sharks and other large fish work side by side with the natives in the harvest. Then, when we in the United States are consuming our Thanksgiving turkey, the Samoans are feasting on delicious baked Palolo epitoke.

The control of the periodicity—which, of course, virtually assures fertilization in a species where gamete union is otherwise left to chance—is not yet understood. Gametes taken from adults will not fuse until 12 h before the time for surface emigration (Mayer, 1902). The stage of the tide over the reef is not involved, as worms isolated in a bucket a day in advance will still carry out the stereotyped spawning ritual (Krämer, 1899). It is not the onset of daylight either, as was shown by Treadwell (1909), who placed worm-bearing coral in darkness the day before the expected rise. These epitokes emerged at the proper time. All this suggests the involvement of a clock, and the laboratory studies of Hauenschild, Fischer, and Hofman (1968) suggest this to be the case.

Korringa (1947) describes unimodal monthly breeding rhythms in two species of mollusks and seven species of annelids. Only one of these rhythms has been tested for persistence in the laboratory and was found not to be clock-controlled (Hauenschild, 1960).

Enright (1972a), you will recall (Chapter 2), found that the daily amount of activity of the amphipod, *Excirolana*, is a function of the day of the month.

Nonmarine Species

As alluded to briefly in Chapter 1, the planaria, *Dugesia dorotocephala*, was found to undergo a monthly rhythm in its orientation to light. In conjunction with experiments designed to test the role of magnetic flux on swimming direction, the worms were placed on a polar grid, illuminated from behind and to the right (Figure 9-10), and the ambient magnetic field altered. Being negatively phototactic, the worms moved into the left quadrant of the grid and their chosen angle was noted when they crossed the arc periphery. As a fringe benefit to finding that organisms have the capacity to orient to a magnetic field, it was also found that the control animals (i.e., those not exposed to a magnetic field) underwent a monthly rhythm in orientation to light (Figure 1-2). During the days centered over new moon the worms deviated significantly to the left of the route assumed around the days of full moon (Brown, 1969). The adaptive significance of this behavior is unknown.

The common hamster, *Mesocricetus auratus*, is another example of a nonmarine animal displaying a monthly rhythm. A 2-yr study of the running-wheel behavior of four male hamsters in LD 12:12, produced the average activity curves shown in Figure 9-11A–B (Brown and Park, 1967). The form of the curves reveals the action of the underlying solar-day clock (as previously described by Brown, 1965), which allows the animals to anticipate the onset of light and darkness.

For each day during the 2-year study, the average daily activity was calculated and these data then reduced to a synodic monthly curve for each year (Figure 9-10A' and B'). While one would have preferred to have the points fall less erratically, the repeatability of the trends during the 2 years is inescapable: the activity peaks just after new and full moons. Since no obvious lunar clues were available to the animals, the

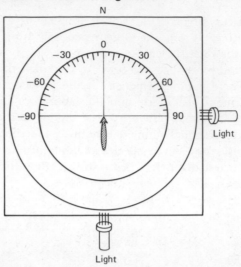

Figure 9-10. Orientational apparatus used to measure the turning response of the flatworm, *Dugesia dorotocephala,* to two point sources of light, one behind and the other to the right of the worm. A single worm is shown at the starting point. Being photonegative, the flatworm swims into the left quadrant, and the angle assumed is noted when the arc is crossed (Brown, Hastings and Palmer, 1970).

modulation of the amount of daily activity into a rhythm must be attributed to an underlying monthly clock.

A case of an *overt* synodic lunar-monthly rhythm is described by Lang (1964, 1967) in the color sensitivity of the guppy, *Lebistes reticulatus.* This little fresh water fish maintains its dorsal–ventral axis parallel to gravity when the fish is maintained in a diffuse or overhead source of light (Figure 9-12A). However, when illuminated by a point source of light from the side, this fish tilts away from vertical toward the light source (Figure 9-12B)—the eventual oblique angle assumed being somewhere between the gravitational and light vectors. The final angle depends on the quality and quantity of the light and—curiously—on the day of month!

To make these measurements, Lang observed his test animals in a horizontal glass cylinder where they were forced to swim against a current of water. The velocity of the latter was regulated so that the fish remained in one place and could be observed head on. The fish was then illuminated from its right side by a xenon lamp with a variety of colored filters, and the degree of lean was measured. The angle assumed was therefore a good measure of the fish's spectral light sensitivity. All meas-

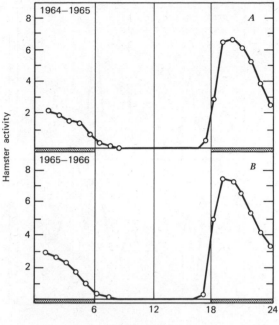

Figure 9-11. The mean daily and synodic monthly activity rhythms of the hamster, *Mesocricetus auratus*. Curves *A* and *B* represent the average hourly activity for two hamsters during 1964–1965 and for two others during 1965–1966, in LD 12:12. The mean daily amount of activity of these animals was also calculated for each day of the synodic month—separately for each year—and illustrated in *A'* and *B'* (next page). It is seen that even though the hamsters received no obvious lunar clues, there was a monthly modulation in the amount of activity that they displayed each day (modified from Brown and Park, 1967).

urements were made at the same time of day, at 2-day intervals for several months.

It was found that the guppy was most sensitive to yellow (583 nm) light during full moon and least responsive around the times of new moon (Figure 9-11C). Just the reverse was true for violet (432 nm) and red (670 nm). The response to other parts of the spectrum were not rhythmic.

Dreisler (1940, 1941) has found that in man the ratio between the sensitivity to green and yellow light also undergoes a monthly rhythm, with the maxima coming during the weeks of full moon.

Serendipity, in conjunction with a study of the initial water uptake

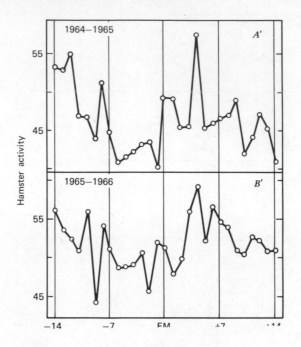

Figure 9-11 (continued)

rates of the pinto bean (*Phaseolus vulgaris*), has brought to light another monthly rhythm. Dried seeds that had previously been stored in CC were placed in water for 4-h (the time always spanning noon), and the weight increase was determined. After a study encompassing two-thirds of a year and involving over 158,000 beans, it was found that the rate of water uptake was a function of the day of the synodic month. As shown in Figure 9–13, the rhythm peaked just before the times of new and full moon and first and last quarter (Brown and Chow, 1973).

In line with the knowledge of monthly breeding cycles in marine organisms, humans have often speculated that the female half of their species may also reflect this frequency. Even the term *menstrual* implies an intentional relationship with the month and the moon. In fact, when Menaker and Menaker (1959) reevaluated the original raw data from which the 28-day average menstrual period was derived (the interval that 9.5 million American women now regulate their cycle to with "the pill"), they claim that the average period is actually 29.5 days—the exact interval of the synodic month. Human gestation, the interval between conception

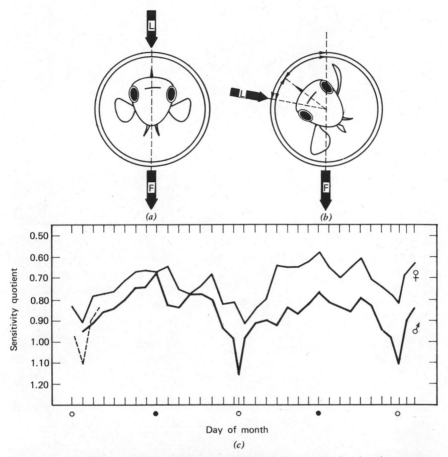

Figure 9-12. The monthly rhythm in yellow-light sensitivity in the guppy, *Lebistes veticulatus*. (A) Orientation angle assumed with light (L) directly overhead (F=gravity). (B) Orientation angle assumed with light to one side. (C) Plots of two guppys' sensitivity to light as determined by dividing the daily response obtained in yellow light into that obtained for white light, to yield the sensitivity quotient. Clearly, the angle adopted is a function of the phase of the moon. Open circles signify the day of the full moon, and solid circles, the new moon (modified from Lang, 1967).

and birth, averages 266 days, exactly 9 synodic months. Counting backward 266 days from the birthdays of over a quarter of a million children born in municipal hospitals in New York City, the same authors also

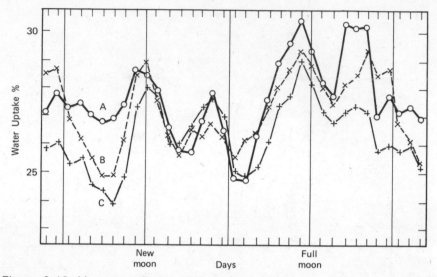

Figure 9-13. Mean synodic monthly pattern of percent water uptake (during first 4 h after inundation) of dried pinto beans (*Phaseolus vulgaris*) for three concurrent, but separate, experiments in 1972. Average curves are smoothed by 3-day moving averages (Brown and Chow, 1973).

found that the conception rate is slightly, but significantly, higher for a few days centered on full moon. Increased conception could signify increased mating activity at this time—a phenomenon quite common to marine animals.

In the same vein, it has always been tacitly assumed that the female libido is probably rhythmic, with the peak times in sexual drive synchronized to ovulation. From an evolutionary point of view, this is a very reasonable supposition, since the association would function to help insure copulatory cooperation between sexes at a time most propitious for species survival. Cavanagh (1969) undertook a formal investigation of this claim. In designing his approach, he discovered that many women volunteers could not be used. He rejected all those who had had hysterectomies, those taking birth-control pills, those who were sexually active and therefore often sated, those who were were frigid, and the fraction "who always felt like sex." His remaining paltry sample contained 30 women, all with regular menstrual cycles, no regular sex life, and all under psychotherapy. At some point during their frequent sessions with the psychotherapist, they were queried about their immediate sexual desires. In this way, waxing and waning patterns in libido titer were

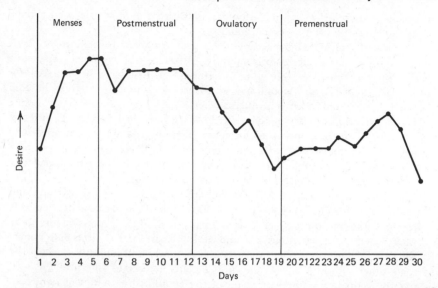

Figure 9-14. The changing monthly desire for sexual intercourse in 30 women over 75 menstrual cycles (drawn from the data of Cavanagh, 1969, and presented in Palmer, 1970).

established over 75 menstrual cycles. As seen in Figure 9-14, Cavanagh found a definite monthly change in desire, characterized by a broad peak burgeoning during menses and spanning the time to ovulation. (Similar studies suggest that women reach orgasmic climax more often around the middle of their menstrual month. This means that the small fraction of women who practice the rhythm method of birth control by abstaining from intercourse until day 21 or 23 deny themselves satisfaction during their peak of desire. This must certainly be a major cause of frustration to them).

SUMMARY AND CONCLUSIONS

1. The moon and sun orientation of several sand-beach amphipods is described. Both displays are clock-controlled, with the desired orientation angle genetically determined.
2. *Fortnightly rhythms:* The persistent gamete liberation rhythms of two algae, *Dictyota dichotoma* and *Halicystis ovalis,* are described. Fortnightly breeding rhythms in animals are very common in nature, but few have ever been tested for persistence in the lab. A fortnightly rhythm is even described in a single isolated cell.

3. Monthly rhythms (or annual rhythms in which the rhythmic event occurs at a definite time of a particular month) :

   A. *Marine forms:* The breeding rhythm of *Eunice,* which in principle is representative of many monthly rhythms, is described. Spawning rhythms are very common in nature, but few have been tested for persistence in the laboratory. The *Excirolana* monthly activity rhythm is known to be clock-controlled.

   B. *Nonmarine forms:* Persistent rhythms are described in planaria orientation, hamster spontaneous locomotor activity, changing color sensitivity in a fish, and water uptake in the bean seed. There also appears to be a rhythm in the libido of the human female, but it is highly speculative whether this is under the control of a living clock.

4. Probably because of the additional amounts of time required to study and repeat observations, very little work has been done on synodic monthly rhythms and the timing mechanisms involved in their expression. In those cases in which the rhythms are known to persist in CC, it is not known whether they are controlled by specific fortnightly and monthly clocks or by some other means. For example, it is equally logical to interpret the fortnightly frequency as the expression of the combined activities of daily and tidal clocks: the daily amplitude simply being reinforced and augmented at 14.7-day intervals by the tidal peak passing over it. Similarly, monthly rhythms could be a composite of the dual activities of solar-day and lunar-day clocks in which the latter would increase the amplitude output of the former at 29.5-day intervals.

Literature Cited

Brown, F. A., Jr. 1965. Propensity for lunar periodicity in hamsters and its significance for biological clock theories. *Proc. Soc. Exper. Biol. Med.,* 120:792–797.

Brown, F. A., Jr. 1969. A hypothesis for extrinsic timing of circadian rhythms. *Can. J. Bot.,* 47:287–298.

Brown, F. A., Jr. and C. S. Chow. 1973. Lunar-correlated variations in water uptake by bean seeds. *Biol. Bull.,* 145:265–278.

Brown, F. A., Jr. and Y. H. Park. 1967. Synodic monthly modulation of the diurnal rhythm of hamsters. *Proc. Soc. Exper. Biol. Med.,* 125:712–715.

Burrows, W. 1945. Periodic spawning of Palolo worms in Pacific waters. *Nature,* 155:47–48.

Cavanagh, J. R. 1969. Rhythm of sexual desire in women. *Med. Aspects Human Sex,* 3:29–39.

Clark, F. N. 1925. The life history of *Leuresthes tenuis,* an Atherine fish with tide controlled spawning habits. *Calif. Fish Game Comm. Bull.,* 10:1–51.

Dresler, A. 1940. Über eine jahreszeitliche Schwankung der spektralen Hellempfindlichkeit. *Licht*, 10:79–82.

Dresler, A. 1941. Die subjective Photometrie farbiger Lichter *Naturwiss.*, 29:225–236.

Enright, J. T. 1972a. A virtuoso isopod. Circa-lunar rhythms and their tidal fine structure. *J. Comp. Physiol.*, 77:141–162.

Enright, J. T. 1972b. When the beachhopper looks at the moon: the moon-compass hypothesis. In S. Galler, K. Schmidt-Koenig, G. Jacobs and R. Belleville, Eds., *Animal Orientation and Navigation*. National Aeronautics and Space Administration, Washington, D.C., pp. 523–555.

Hauenschild, C. 1960. Lunar periodicity. *Cold Spring Harbor Symp. Quant. Biol.*, 25:491–497.

Hauenschild, C. A. Fischer, and D. Hofmann. 1968. Untersuchungen am pazifischen Palolowurm *Eunice viridis* (Polychaeta) in Samoa. *Helgolander wiss. Meeresunters*, 18:254–295.

Hollenberg, G. J. 1936. A study of *Halicystis ovalis*. II. Periodicity in the formation of gametes. *Amer. J. Bot.*, 23:1–3.

Hoyt, W. D. 1907. Periodicity in the production of the sexual cells of *Dictyota dichotoma*. *Bot. Gaz.*, 43:383–392.

Hoyt, W. D. 1927. The periodic fruiting of *Dictyota* and its relation to the environment. Amer. *J. Bot.*, 14:592–619.

Keeble, F. 1910. *Plant Animals*. Cambridge University Press, Cambridge.

Klapow, L. A. 1972. Fortnightly molting and reproductive cycles in the sand-beach isopod, *Excirolana chiltoni*. *Biol. Bull.*, 143:568–591.

Korringa, P. 1947. Relations between the moon and periodicity in the breeding of marine animals. *Ecol. Monogr.*, 17:347–381.

Krämer, A. 1899. Palolountersuchungen im Oktober und November 1898 in Samoa. *Biol. Centralb.*, 19:237–239.

Lang, H.-J. 1964. Über lunarperiodische Schwankeungen der Farbempfindlichkeit beim Guppy (*Lebistes reticulatus*). *Verh. dt. zool. Ges.*, 58:379–386.

Lang, H.-J. 1967. Über das Lichtrückenverhalten des Guppy (*Lebistes reticulatus*) in farbigen und farblosen Lichtern. *Z. vergl. Physiol.*, 56:296–340.

Lowe, C. D. Hinds, P. Lardner, and K. Justice. 1967. Natural free-running period in vertebrate animal populations. *Science*, 156:531–534.

Mayer, A. G. 1902. The Atlantic Palolo. *Sci. Bull. Mus. Brooklyn Inst. Arts Sci.*, 1:93–103.

Menaker, W., and A. Menaker. 1959. Lunar periodicity in human reproduction: a likely unit of biological time. *Amer. J. Obst. Gynec.*, 77:905–914.

Müller, D. 1962. Über jahres- und lunarperiodische Erscheinungen bei einigen Braunalgen. *Bot. Mar.*, 4:140–155.

Page, J. Z., and B. M. Sweeney. 1968. Culture studies on the marine green alga *Halicystis parvula—Derbesia tenuissima.* III. Control of gamete formation by an endogenous rhythm. *J. Phycol.*, 4:253–260.

Palmer, J. D. 1970. The living clocks of man. *Nat. Hist.*, 74 (4):53–59.

Papi, F. 1955. Experiments on the sense of time in *Talitrus saltator* (Montagu) (Crustacea-Amphipoda) *Experientia*, 11:201.

Papi, F. 1960. Orientation by night: the moon. *Cold Spring Harbor Symp. Quant. Biol.*, 25:475–480.

Papi, F., and L. Pardi. 1959. Nuovi reperti sull'orientamento lunare di *Talitrus saltator. Z. vergl. Physiol.*, 41:583–596.

Pardi, L. 1960. Innate components in the solar orientation of littoral amphipods. *Cold Spring Harbor Symp. Quant. Biol.*, 25:395–401.

Stephens, G. C. 1962. Circadian melanophore rhythms of the fiddler crab: interaction between animals. *Ann. N.Y. Acad. Sci.*, 98:926–939

Strumwasser, F. 1965. The demonstration and manipulation of a circadian rhythm in a single neuron. In J. Aschoff, Ed., *Circadian Clocks*. North-Holland Publ. Co., Amsterdam, pp. 442–462.

Thompson, W. F. 1919. The spawning of the grunion (*Leuresthes tenuis*). *Calif. Fish Game Comm. Bull.*, 3:1–29.

Treadwell, A. L. 1909. *Annelids of Tortugas*. Yearbook No. 8, Carnegie Institute, Washington.

Vielhaben, V. 1963. Zur Deutung des semilunaren Fortpflanzungszyklus von *Dictyota dichotoma. Z. Bot.*, 51:156–173.

Williams, J. L. 1905. Studies in the dictyotaceae. III. The periodicity of the sexual cells in *Dictyota dichotoma. Ann. Bot.*, 19:531–560.

Woodworth, W. McM. 1903. The Palolo worm, *Eunice viridis* (Gray). *Bull. Mus. Comp. Zool. Harvard Univ.*, 51:3–21.

10 The Clock Underlying Persistent Rhythms

Because so much more is known about the clocks controlling circadian rhythms, we will begin the discussion with them.

LOCATION IN THE ORGANISM

A clock (or possibly more than one) is thought to reside in each cell of a multicellular organism or in each individual in a population of unicells. This fact has been documented many times. For example, Sweeney (1960), in a delicately intricate experiment, demonstrated that the photosynthetic rhythm of the dinoflagellate *Gonyaulax* persisted in an individual cell isolated in a Cartesian diver. Other examples are isolated hearts and heart cells that continue to undergo a daily rhythm in rate of beat (Tharp and Folk, 1964); the daily rhythm in spontaneous impulse activity of isolated neurons (Chapter 9; Strumwasser, 1965; Jacklet, 1969); and *Acetabularia* cells, which continue to describe daily wave forms in their photosynthetic pattern—even after enucleation (Figure 10-1) (Sweeney and Haxo, 1961). Quite obviously, the clock exists at the cellular level in these organisms. The same conclusion is forthcoming from experiments that demonstrate that rhythms persist in small, isolated multicellular segments of large organisms. Examples are carrot tissue explants that continue to display turgor-pressure rhythms (Enderle, 1951); isolated hamster intestine contracts rhythmically (Bünning, 1958); isolated hamster adrenals continue their secretion rhythms (Andrews & Folk, 1963; Andrews, 1967); and the CO_2-output rhythm persists in segregated mesophyll (Wilkins, 1959).

In some cases at the multicellular level of organization, a clock located in one region of the body is known to exert a temporal control over a process elsewhere in the organism, extending its influence via hormonal substances (Harker, 1954, 1956; Truman, 1971) or neurally (Brady, 1969, 1971). In Chapters 2, 4, and 5, you will remember that removal of the eyestalks (an important hormone producing site) of some crabs

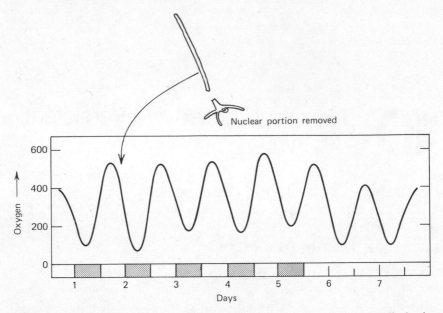

Figure 10-1. The photosynthetic-capacity rhythm in the single-celled alga *Acetabularia*. Oxygen-liberation measurements made under identical light intensities of equal duration, but at different times of day, revealed that the capacity to undergo photosynthesis was greater during the daytime than at night. This rhythm persisted even after the cell was enucleated on day 2 and placed in LL on day 6 (drawn from the data of Sweeney and Haxo, 1961).

stopped rhythmic activity in locomotion, color change, and oxidative metabolism. (En passant, one should mention that no matter how interesting the experiments on the nervous and hormonal control of rhythms, they really add little to our understanding of the fundamental clock mechanism—as described above, the clock does not need the endocrine or neural levels of organization to function.)

DETERMINATION OF PHASE AND PERIOD

In the natural habitat, potential circadian rhythms are entrained to the ambient day–night cycle and thus have periods precisely restricted to 24 h. The proper phase adjustment to ambient LD cycles is primarily brought about by illumination of an underlying light-sensitive *phase-setting rhythm* (DeCoursey, 1961, 1964). This rhythm is fairly constant in "idea of form" from organism to organism (Figure 10-2) and is observed as a response curve that illustrates the amount and direction of phase change that will be produced by a light stimulus. [A similar temperature-sensitive rhythm (Figure 8-1) (Stephens, 1957; Moser, 1962; Zimmerman, Pittendrigh, and Pavlidis, 1968) plays, to a lesser extent, the same role.] Figure 10-3 diagrammatically describes the role of a phase-setting rhythm in the enterainment of an organismic oscillation to an LD cycle.

In the constant conditions of the laboratory situation, these two phase-setting rhythms continue to function (both are active in LL, while only the temperature-sensitivity one functions in DD) and attempt to bring the experimental organism's rhythms into the proper phase relationship with the new conditions. They do this by producing a small phase change each "day," which, if the net change is a phase advance, shortens the period for that day or, if it is a phase delay, lengthens the period. In these very unnatural conditions, where daylight and warmth do not alternate with cool darkness, a satisfactory phase relationship can never be achieved; the phase-change mechanism continues to cause phase alterations eternally, producing as an inevitable consequence a change in the period of the organism's overt rhythm (Figure 10-4). This response has been termed "autophasing" (Brown, 1972). Therefore, in CC, the period displayed is a relatively constant interval falling—most often—somewhere between 22 and 26 h rather than the monotonous 24-h period displayed in nature. In LL or DD and depending on the level of constant light and/or temperature, the ultimate length of the period assumed is a function of the *form* (Figure 10-2) of the light or temperature phase-setting rhythms, respectively. In fact, the temperature resetting rhythm is probably responsible for the slight "temperature-dependent" changes in the period that cause the temperature coefficient to deviate slightly from unity (Chapter 8); in other words, the clock could be completely temperature-independent and its driven rhythms still show alterations in period because of temperature changes. Any sudden change in the form of an individual's phase-response curve would bring about an immediate "spontaneous" change in the overt period of the organism's rhythm (Palmer, 1964).

Recognizing the period distorting action in CC of the light- and temperature-sensitivity rhythms is very important. Assuming that each "automatic" phase change is analogous to resetting the hands of one's clock, it becomes apparent that the overt period shown to the observer by his experimental organism in CC is usually different from the "natural" period of the bioclock underlying the rhythm. A form of "uncertainty principal" applies here because as long as the phase-setting mechanism is functioning, the clock's true period can never be precisely known to the investigator.

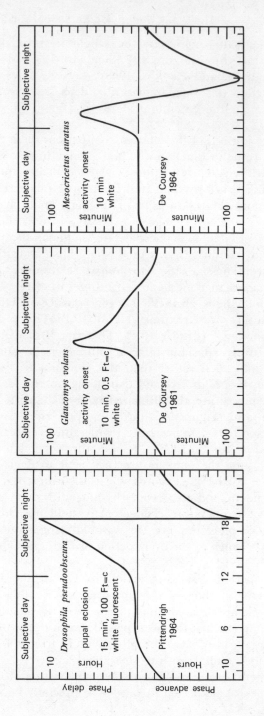

Figure 10.1.

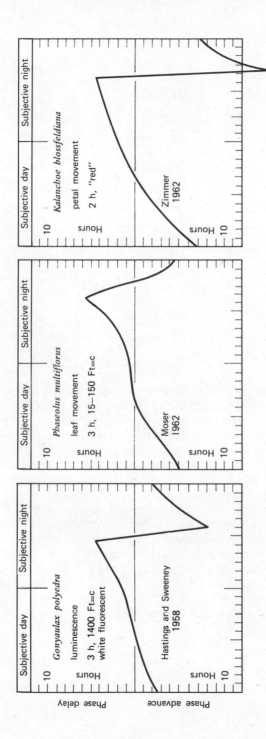

Figure 10-2. Light-pulse-produced phase-response rhythm for six different organisms. From left to right, top row: fruit fly, flying squirrel, hamster; bottom row: dinoflagellate, bean, house plant. As can be seen, in general a light pulse given during the first portion of the subjective night (i.e., what had been the hours of darkness prior to transfer to CC) produces phase delays, while the identical treatment in the latter half produces phase advances. During the subjective day (ie, the light portion of LD regimen prior to transfer to CC) the phase shift, if any, is usually minor. Type of rhythm, duration and intensity of light pulse, and original reference, are indicated next to each curve (modified from Pittendrigh, 1965).

131

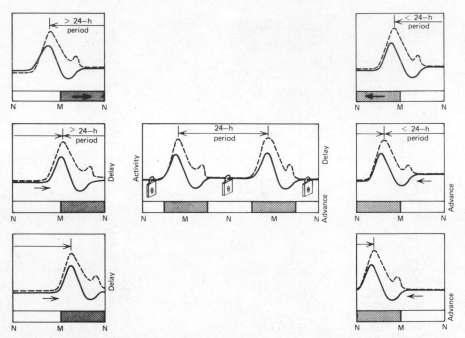

Figure 10-3. The role of a phase-setting rhythm in adjusting a clock-driven rhythm to a 12:12 light-dark cycle. Center: the dashed curve represents a nocturnal overt rhythm "locked" to an underlying light-sensitive phase-setting rhythm (solid line). Because of the action of the latter, the peaks of the overt rhythm are confined to the period of darkness signified by the shaded portions along the abscissa. To illustrate the way a resetting rhythm functions, the dark portion of a laboratory LD cycle is made to begin 6 h later (upper left-hand corner) than in center diagram, which then exposes the delay portion of the phase-setting rhythm to light. This produces, by the next day (middle left), a delay in the peak of the overt rhythm. These delays are continually caused until the old desired nocturnal phase relationship again obtains (bottom left). The vertical series on the right-hand side of the diagram illustrates a similar phase adjustment, but in this case the dark period has been *advanced* by 6 h, thus exposing the advance segment of the resetting rhythm. Consequently, after a series of phase advances, the overt rhythm is again centered in the hours of darkness (bottom right). (N=noon; M=midnight.)

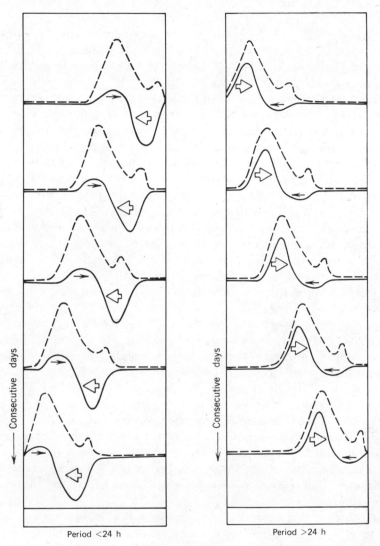

Period <24 h   Period >24 h

Figure 10-4. The action of a light-sensitive phase-setting rhythm in the laboratory. In LL, both the advance and delay portions of the resetting rhythm are
illuminated and the net amount and direction of "daily" resetting is determined by the relative effects of these two portions. Therefore, the phase
change produced is a function of the form of the resetting rhythm. The
form on the left produces phase advances, while that on the right produces
delays. In the absence of LD cycles, the resetting rhythm cannot ever "find"
the proper phase relationship with nighttime, so the search lasts eternally,
and, as a consequence, produces a *circadian* period.

THE COUPLER BETWEEN CLOCK AND DRIVEN PROCESS

A great deal of evidence points to the fact that the clock driving circadian rhythms is an entity in itself, being quite distinct from the overt process that it causes to be rhythmic. For example, a photosynthetic inhibitor such as dichlorophenyl dimethyl urea, when pulsed into the dinoflagellate *Gonyaulax,* will temporarily stop photosynthesis, yet the photosynthetic rhythms will commence again in phase with controls when the substance is removed. Pulsed puromycin inhibits bioluminescence in the same organism, and again on removal, the luminescent rhythm restarts in phase with the control (summarized in Brown, Hastings, and Palmer, 1970). Moderately low temperature pulses stop locomotion in the green crab, but on rewarming, the rhythm in activity is renewed, again in phase with the controls (Chapter 7). Clearly, in these cases the clock has continued to run, even though no overt rhythms were displayed, showing the clock is not part (i.e., a rhythmic step) of either the photosynthetic or bioluminescent processes or an intrinsic feature of locomotion. Instead, it is an entity distinct from these processes but connected to them in some way via a coupling mechanism, causing them to be rhythmic.

As suggested by Dowse and Palmer (1972), at least two types of hypothetical coupling mechanisms can be imagined: direct and indirect. By direct coupling is meant some relatively simple, inflexible means of attachment between clock and driven process (Figure 10-5, right-hand side). Among the forms of indirect coupling is the possibility of a separate coupling entity, interpolated between the clock and driven process (Figure 10-5, left-hand side). One of the properties of this latter type of coupler is its ability to function as a phase and frequency transformer. There are several reasons for believing that a coupling mechanism of the indirect type just described does exist. In the following description, it is assumed that the cell possesses a single master horologe that drives all the cell's rhythms.

The existence of a distinct coupler entity would explain in an uncomplicated way the simultaneous existence of different circadian frequencies in the same organism, as has been found in the petal-movement and fragrance rhythms of *Cestrum* (periods of 27 and 29 h, respectively, in identical CC) (Overland, 1960); in the growth rhythms of the oat coleoptile and primary leaf (periods of 24 and 24.75, respectively, in CC) (Ball and Newcombe, 1961); and in a few of the many rhythms of man (Lobban, 1965; Aschoff, Gerecke, and Wever, 1967; Aschoff, 1969). A frequency-transforming coupling mechanism for each rhythmic process, connected to a single clock, would produce these results. The possibility

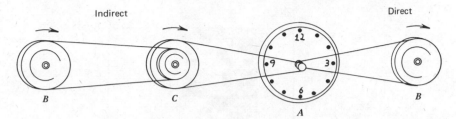

Figure 10-5. A belt-driven pulley analogy representing two means of coupling between a "biological" clock (A) and the process it causes to be rhythmic (B). The right-hand paradigm illustrates direct coupling by a pulley belt, and the left-hand one by an interposed coupling pulley (C). The relative diameters of the compound pulley function to alter the frequency being transmitted from the clock to the process. Several different rhythmic processes, each differing in frequency and phase, could be driven by the same clock if each process had its own "indirect" coupler (Dowse and Palmer, 1972).

also exists that a single coupler may act as an intermediate for more than one rhythm in some cases, an idea that is suggested by the results of Konopka and Benzer (1971) and will be described later in the discussion of the gene control of rhythms.

MASTER OR MULTIPLE CLOCKS?

Many species are known to display several- rhythms simultaneously: in man more that 50 rhythms are known to exist (Conroy and Mills, 1970), and in a less complex organism, *Gonyaulax*, 4 separate rhythmic processes have been described (McMurry and Hastings, 1972). The question arises as to whether a single master clock drives all the rhythms or whether each rhythm is governed by its own clock. Because the means of coupling between clock and driven process is unknown, the question cannot be resolved at present. However, evidence from one organism has been construed to indicate that a single clock drives all the individual's rhythms.

Studies of the four known rhythms (luminescence capacity, "glow," photosynthesis, and cell division) of *Gonyaulax* have produced the following findings; (1) All four rhythms have the same temperature coefficient (an unusual one of about 0.85). (2) All are simultaneously phase-shifted in the same direction and amount by a single dark or dim light pulse given at any one time. (3) The phase relationships between the rhythms do not change after lengthy sojourns in CC (as they would be expected to do if each was controlled by its own clock, any of which ran at an even slightly different rate). McMurry and Hastings (1972) cautiously point out that the similarity in the responses of the four

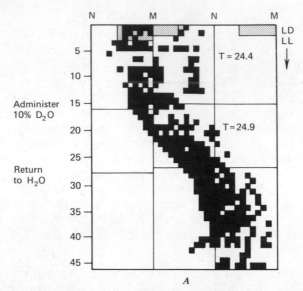

Figure 10-6 (A). Representative example of the altering by D_2O of the period of the mouse (*Mus musculus*) locomotor rhythm. The dark blocks represent times of major daily activity; the stippling signifies the hours of darkness. The ordinate shows consecutive days, and the abscissa, hours. (A) At point LL, the mouse was switched from LD 12:12 (8) to constant light (0.2 ft-c) and the period of its persistent rhythm determined (to be about 24.4 h) over the next 13 days. For the next 12 days it was permitted to drink only 10% D_2O, which lengthened the period to 24.9 h. The mouse was then given completely proteated water again, which caused the period to revert to a value close to the starting one. For graphic clarity, the abscissa has been extended to the right beyond 24 h (excerpted from Dowse and Palmer, 1972).

rhythms to dark pulses and temperature, and their lack of phase drift in CC, are "consistent with the hypothesis that the rhythms are all outputs of a single master oscillator."

An alternate interpretation can be arrived at deductively as follows: That the four rhythms in *Gonyaulax* have the same temperature coefficients signifies that the temperature phase-setting rhythms for the four are identical. That a single pulse of darkness produces the same phase change in all rhythms means that they have identical light-sensitive phase-setting rhythms that are all in phase. Therefore, if both the temperature and light phase-setting rhythms are identical, the fact that all 4 rhythms stay in phase for extended durations in CC is mandatory and does not necessarily provide any direct statement about the clock (s).

RESISTANCE TO CHEMICAL RESETTING

An unusual feature of a living horologe is its near complete immunity

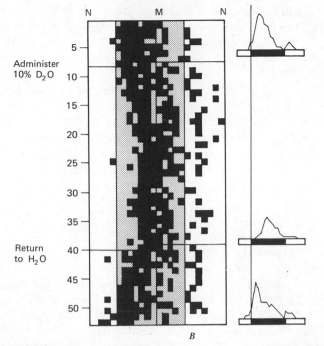

Figure 10-6 (B). Representitive example of the altering by D_2O of the phase of the mouse locomotor rhythm. The mouse, maintained in LD 12:12 (8) throughout the study, was given 10% D_2O on day 9; the concentration produced a 2–3 h phase delay (see X daily form-estimate curves on right ordinate). A few days after return to regular water the old phase relationship was re-established (excerpted from Dowse and Palmer, 1972).

to a whole host of chemical inhibitors, narcotizing agents, growth stimulants, antimetabolites, and other types of sustained or pulsed chemical insults. In fact, the generalization arising from a great many studies is that the clock is virtually invulnerable to exogenous chemical permutations. Some workers have even philosophized that this insensitivity would be an expected property, since accuracy under any conditions is probably the most important feature of all clocks. However, chemical immutability is not a property of other pacemaker systems.

Recently, two substances have been found that consistently alter biological rhythms: they are deuterium oxide (Bruce and Pittendrigh, 1960; Bünning and Baltes, 1963; Suter and Rawson, 1968; Palmer and Dowse, 1969; Enright, 1971a; Dowse and Palmer, 1972) and ethyl alcohol (Keller, 1960; Enright, 1971b). The cronomutagenic effect of D_2O is particularly interesting in that it will alter both the period (in a dose-dependent fashion) and the phase of a rhythm, as shown in Figure 10-6 (Dowse and Palmer, 1972). Unfortunately, the effects of heavy water on living systems are so manifold that its specific influence on the clock cannot as yet be ascertained. Also, the very distinct possibility exists that D_2O is exerting its effect not on the clock per se but on the coupling mechanism.

In a similar manner, cycloheximide (an inhibitor of protein synthesis) has also been shown to alter the period of a rhythm. However, other than the original paper (Feldman, 1967), one informally reported confirming study that qualified some of the former results (mentioned in Enright, 1971b), and two negative reports (Sargent, 1969; Enright, 1971b), apparently no serious work with cycloheximide has been undertaken.

INNATENESS OF THE CLOCK

The period of a daily rhythm is neither learned nor is it imprinted on organisms by day–night cycles of light and temperature. Instead, the capacity for rhythmicity is innate. The confirming evidence for this comes from three lines of experimentation: (1) Semon (1905) germinated seeds of *Acacia lophantha*—a plant known to undergo a sleep-movement rhythm (the leaves are raised to the sun during the day and lowered to the stem at night)—in LD 6:6 or LD 24:24. In spite of the fact that the plants were under these extreme "days" and had never seen a true day, the leaves raised and lowered with a period approaching 24 h, and this period persisted when they were switched to LL (dim). (2) Chickens (Aschoff and Meyer-Lohman, 1954) and lizards (Hoffman, 1957) were raised from eggs in CC. When placed in actographs, their activity patterns were found to have become circadian de novo—that is, without the animals ever experiencing a single day–night cycle. (3) The last example comes from the fruit fly, *Drosophila*. This pest displays an eclosion rhythm (i.e., it emerges from its pupal case only around dawn), and a population of pupae moved to CC continues this pattern. However, if batches of eggs are laid and made to develop in CC, the resulting adults emerge at all times of the day. Fifteen generations of flies were made to remain arrhythmic by keeping them in DD until finally a light was turned on and left on; this simple alteration in illumination (which provided no information on period) acted as the stimulus to reestablish rhythmicity to the entire pupulation (Bünning, 1935a). [Recall also in Chapter 2 (Figure 2-15) that a single temperature pulse similarly started the green crab tidal activity rhythm.] Therefore, it is obvious that the ability to measure off periods of 24 h in length is a deep-seated property of protoplasm. So deep in fact that not even being sheltered from day–night cycles for 15 generations—or possibly even more deceptive, being made to believe that full "days" were really as little as 12 or as much as 48 hours long—could modify the fundamental ∼24-h innate period.

Recognizing the innateness of the capacity for rhythmicity, a series of genetic studies have been carried out. The findings fall into three categories: (1) Back-crosses between rhythmic mutants and nonrhythmic wild type *Neurospora crassa* (Stadler, 1959; Sussman, Lowry, and Durkee, 1964) or the protozoan *Paramecium multimicronucleatum* (Barnett, 1966) have shown that the rhythmic trait segregates in a 1:1 ratio signifying that the mutation occurred at a single gene locus. Results such as these could mean that the clock has been directly affected, but it is equally likely that the lack of rhythmicity simply signifies an absence of coupling between clock and driven process. This latter idea is strengthened by finding that in two clones of *P. multimicronucleatum*, both of which display persistent circadian cell-division rhythms, the gene-controlled rhythm of mating reversal is missing in one clone (Barnett, 1969). This suggests that the difference between clones is the presence or absence of the coupler for the mating rhythm: certainly the clock is present in both strains. (2) The phase relationship maintained between rhythms and the ambient light-lark cycle has also been shown to be determined genetically in the *Paramecium* mating-reversal rhythm (Barnett, 1966) and in the *Drosophila* eclosion rhythm (Pittendrigh, 1967; Clayton and Paietta, 1972). In the latter case, flies that eclosed very early or very late during the daily emergence peak were systematically isolated and bred with their own kind. After 50 generations of artificial selection, a 4-h difference in phase phenotype existed. (3) The period also appears to be genetically controlled. This was first suggested by the pioneering work of Bünning (1935b), in which he crossed individual bean plants whose persistent sleep-movement rhythms had periods that differed significantly from each other when maintained in identical CC. He found that the first generation offspring displayed intermediate periods. Konopka and Benzer (1971) induced mutants in *Drosophila melanogaster* and found that 3 of 2000 mutant candidates screened had altered rhythms: the first had a period of 28 h, the second had a period of only 19 h, and the third was arrhythmic. The periods of both the eclosion and activity rhythms of these animals were lengthened or shortened identically. Mapping traced all these altered phenotypes to one functional gene on the X chromosome. Bruce (1972) has similarly isolated a long-period mutant of *Chlamydomonas reinhardi*. The fact that the periods of these rhythms have been lengthened or shortened has customarily been interpreted to mean that the basic horologe has been altered. More accurately, since it is the forms of the phase-setting rhythms that control the period length in CC, it is these that have probably been directly altered by the mutation. Carrying the speculation one step farther and invoking the phase–frequency-transforming coupler hypothesis, and remembering that this is the unit responsible for the overt period displayed to the experimenter, it is this unit that may have suffered the consequences of the genetic change. That both the eclosion and activity rhythms were altered identically suggests that both may be under the mediation of a single frequency-transducing coupler.

THE NATURE OF THE CLOCK

To date, the postulated clock underlying rhythms has not been localized or characterized. All working hypotheses concerning its nature fall into one of two general types (Figure 10-7): (1) those positing an escapement-type clock that exists within the cells of organisms and gen-

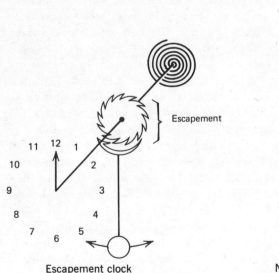

Figure 10-7. Diagrammatic comparison of escapement and nonescapement clocks. In the former, the energy provided by the spring is released in identical packages at uniformly spaced intervals via the escapement mechanism and swinging pendulum. Therefore, this type of clock generates its own interval of time. That is not the case with the sundial, which simply indicates the interval information transmitted to it by an exogenous source.

erates its own time interval autonomously, or (2) those positing a nonescapement-type clock, also present in cells but receiving its timing information from some periodic environmental force capable of penetrating the confines of so-called constant conditions.* For a detailed summary of these views see Brown, Hastings, and Palmer (1970); here we will only briefly review them.

The Escapement-Type Clock Hypothesis

The central dogma of this hypothesis is that the basic frequency of the horologe is independently derived (i.e., the clock generates its own period). It is thought that after eons of living under day–night cycles, a protoplasmic clock evolved whose period closely matched that of the environment. The clock proved to be an aid to survival in that it "notified" its owner in *advance* of coming periodic environmental events, such as nightfall or some other important daily eventuality. It is, of course, not known at what epoch clock capability first arose, but the widespread distribution of rhythms throughout the plant and animal kingdom suggests it was an early innovation. If this were the case, occasional readjustment of the period would be necessary to compensate for the reduction in angular momentum of the earth: days have become 3 h longer in the last 600 million yr. If, as some people feel, driven rhythms truly approximate the clock's basic period, then to keep the clock up to date would have required an average slowing down to 18 μsec/yr. If this lengthening of the period did not occur, the same end could have been reached by adopting a frequency-transforming coupler.

The widespread distribution of rhythms (which are apparently present in all life forms but procaryotes; but see Rogers and Greenbank, 1930; Ogate, Nishi, and Yabe, 1955) could either signify that the property arose in a very early stem group and, being of such fundamental importance, was carried on to subsequent branch groups; or, this temporal property arose independently in diverse groups. The fact that all rhythms show the same properties (general insensitivity to temperature change and chemical imposition, entrainment by light and temperature cycles, free run in CC, etc.) is not necessarily an indication that the clockworks of all organisms are identical in makeup. Recognizing that the two most important properties of all good clocks are accuracy under any conditions and the maintenance of a proper relative phase relationship with the

---

* The escapement—nonescapement terminology is preferable to the more commonly used endogenous–exogenous divisions: both types of clocks are obviously influenced by rhythmic *exogenous* factors such as light and temperature cycles; and an exogenous clock must have an *endogenous* receiving unit. Ignoring these facts has been a source of occasional confusion in the past.

environment, then the above properties would be expected to have arisen in conjunction with any type of clock evolved.

Two lines of evidence do suggest that divergent, rather than convergent, evolution may have taken place. Apparently all organisms' phases adjust in the same way: via phase-setting rhythms. Certainly there are a variety of other ways in which phase-setting could be accomplished, so the singleness weakly supports a common origin. [On the other hand, the fact that some organisms undergo transients (see Glossary) and others do not suggests a fundamental difference in the phase-setting mechanisms of different species.] The other suggestion arises from the fact that the clocks (although it may only be the couplers) of a vascular plant, a microorganism, an invertebrate, and several vertebrate species all react in a virtually identical way to treatment with deuterium oxide.

An argument often used in the past in support of an escapement-type living clock is based on the presence of a non–24-hour period of rhythms in CC. It was proffered that these frequencies represented the connate period of the clock, which was masked in the natural setting by LD cycles that entrained the rhythm to a strict 24-h periodicity. Because the period in CC is other than 24 h and all impinging geophysical forces that pervade experimental conditions have strict 24-h periods, then the circadian periods could not derive from the pervasive environment. We are now aware (or should be) that because of the phase-setting rhythms the period displayed in CC does not necessarily reflect the basic clock period.

Arguments against the escapement idea are as follow: The two factors that most complicate this hypothesis are the virtual temperature-independence of the period and insensitivity to a wide variety of chemical perturbations. The clock, as an internal biochemical entity, would not be expected to have these properties. Having them requires the addition to the hypothesis of compensating explanations—a necessity but a violation of the tenets of Occam's razor. Additionally, the clock has not been located within the cell. Even cells in which the nucleus has been removed (Figure 10-1) have been observed to remain rhythmic for as long as 40 days in CC (Schweiger, Wallraff, and Schweiger, 1964). It is true, however, that these cells (*Acetabularia*) are richly supplied with chloroplastic and mitochondrial DNA, which may at least partially compensate in the absence of the nucleus. But DNA is not necessarily involved in timing, as has been demonstrated in dormant onion seeds (a stage in the life cycle in which DNA replication, transcription, and translation are not detectable), which have been shown to undergo a temperature-independent nocturnal rhythm in oxidative metabolism in DD

(Bryant, 1972). Another problem is the duplication of the clock during cell division without a loss in accuracy. The depth of this problem is dramatically emphasized in a cleverly designed experiment by Barnett (1965). She moved 8 unicells (*Paramecium multimicronucleatum*) from LD to CC, where they then remained for the next 6 days. During this time, they divided to form 121,800 cells. On the seventh day, they were examined for periodicity and their mating-reversal rhythm was found to be intact. This means that the rhythmic capacity arising from the 8 cells —the only ones that had ever "seen" LD cycles—had passed from cell to cell, through 2.2 cell divisions every 24 h, without any loss in accuracy —a truly amazing feat!

The Nonescapement-Type Clock Hypothesis

Properties often cited in support of exogenous timing are the temperature-independence of the period; the spontaneous change of phase in CC occurring after some translocation experiments (Chapter 6); the existence of certain correlations between environmental factors and rhythms in CC (Figure 5-3) (Brown, 1960); the general immunity of the period to chemical perturbation (in the few cases where chemical alteration has been possible it is just as likely that the coupler, rather than the clock, was the unit altered); and, as discussed in Chapter 1, the fact that only rhythms with periods distributed closely around basic geophysical periods have all the clock properties previously described.

The most common objection (Aschoff, 1960; Hoffmann, 1960; Pittendrigh, 1961; Conroy and Mills, 1970) to the nonescapement hypothesis has been that a geophysically cued "daily" clock should produce rhythms that have fundamental periods of 24 or 24.8 h, since geophysical forces impinging on the earth's surface undergo primary oscillations at these two intervals. Yet persistent rhythms are usually circadian or circatidal. As discussed earlier, this argument is easily countered: because of the transmutating effect of the response system employed in phase-shifting, any basic clock period will be altered in CC. It has also been stated (Sweeney, 1963) that the slight temperature-dependence of the period of circadian rhythms is difficult to reconcile with exogenous timing. Again, this dependence could be wholly the effect of different constant temperatures on the temperature-sensitive phase-setting mechanism.

At present, the geophysical force (s) postulated to time rhythms has not been identified. But in the search for it (and for that suspected to be used by animals in orientation) many environmental parameters previously not thought to influence biological systems have been found to do so. For example, cosmic-ray showers (Brown, Bennett, and Ralph,

1955), gamma radiation (Brown and Park, 1964; Brown, Park, and Zeno, 1966; Brown and Webb, 1968), electrostatic fields (Brown, 1962b; Dowse and Palmer, 1969), geomagnetic fields (Brown, 1962a; Palmer, 1963; Brown and Park, 1965; Bennett and Huguenin, 1969; Keeton, 1971; Wiltschko and Wiltschko, 1972), and electromagnetic fields (Wever, 1967, 1969; Brown, 1971; Brown and Chow, 1973) are all known to produce measurable changes in organismic behavior and physiology. All of these forces are periodic and penetrating, thus having the potential to act as exogenous inputs to a nonescapement-type clock. None of them are routinely screened from standard "constant" conditions. It is also possible that the time-giving force may not even be known to science yet.

There is also a distressing quality in the nonescapement hypothesis: while it is testable and can be proved (within the limits of the scientific method), it cannot be disproved. If, after intense and sustained experimentation, the elusive zeitgeber is not found, the lack of success can always be blamed on poor hunting (the same can also be said for not finding an escapement-type clock) rather than on the reality of the force. After all, the force may not even be known to physics yet. The expensive potential exists, of course, to rocket experimental organisms into deep space, away from the earth's rhythmic environment, but how far must the spaceship travel before concluding that it is truly beyond the reach of these forces? [The rhythms of earth-orbiting astronauts were found to persist for 14 real days (while being subjected by the orbital flight to 224 "days" of 90 min); however, the LD cycles in the cabin were normal 24-h ones (Rummel, Sallin, and Lipscomb, 1966).] Therefore, being invulnerable to disproof, proof is the only recourse. Since this leaves but a 50% chance of success to an experimenter willing to accept the challenge of this hypothesis, since most biologists lack geophysical expertise, and since the hypothesis itself has the connotation of a retrograde path from science to astrology, the curiosity of most potential investigators is damped. As a consequence, the nonescapement cartel is a small, but audible, fraction of biochronologists.

Conclusions

It should be recognized that neither the escapement hypothesis nor the nonescapement hypothesis is yet supported by sufficient evidence to choose one over the other; in fact, most of the data thus far accumulated support both equally well. It is also useless to appeal to expert opinion in this problem, since the doyens of both sides are accomplished and respected investigators and theoreticians. It may be that the final answer will be a combination of the two views. All one can do is wait or work.

THE BASIC PERIOD OF CLOCK-CONTROLLED
TIDAL RHYTHMS

Since a clock with a period of about a day in length is thought to underlie daily rhythms, similar logic would dictate that a clock with a period of 12.4 h controls tidal rhythms. This may be the case, but an alternate representation is suggested by much of the evidence: it may be that tidal rhythms are best described as bimodal lunar-day rhythms and are controlled by a lunar-day clock (Palmer, 1973). Evidence suggestive of this follows.

Several organismic tidal rhythms mimic the semidiurnal inequality of the tides (Figure 1-7); that is, they display alternating peaks of large and small amplitude in CC (Figures 2-14; 2-17). This form would be unexpected if a 12.4-h clock produced each rhythmic wave. A hypothesis based on a 12.4-h clock would have to contain, in addition, some adjusting mechanism that either suppresses or amplifies alternate peaks (just as a grandfather clock would have to have an additional mechanism if it was to chime more loudly during the daytime hours). However, the inequality is more easily explained by postulating an underlying lunar-day clock (i.e., a horologe with a basic period close to 24.8 h) that produces a bimodal lunar-day rhythm with an asymmetrical form. This scheme is directly analogous to circadian clocks, which often produce activity rhythms in CC with a major peak at the time just after subjective sunrise and a second, lesser peak just before subjective sunset (Figure 1-3).

As described in Chapter 7, green crabs were made to be arrhythmic by protracted storage in CC and then subjected to alternating high–low pressure cycles. Although the pressure cycles were of equal amplitude, the rhythm they induced in the crabs contained a semidiurnal inequality in peak height (Figure 7-7b). This indicates that the form of the rhythm may be innate. However, I must emphasize here that two different situations obtain with regard to the semidiurnal inequality in amplitude of living rhythms. In one case, as just discussed above and diagrammed in Figure 10-8A, the unequal nature of the peakedness apparently is a characteristic of the lunar-day clock underlying the rhythms. In cases like these the unequal pattern may be embossed on the organism by the tidal environment [as has been shown in *Excirolana* (Figures 2-8; 7-4)]. In the more usual case, whichever peak falls within a particular fraction of the solar day is reduced (or amplified, as the case may be) (Figure 10-8B). Since the pattern often persists in CC, it is thought to be the combined manifestation of the interaction of solar-day and lunar-day clocks, the former distorting at least one tidal peak per solar day (much

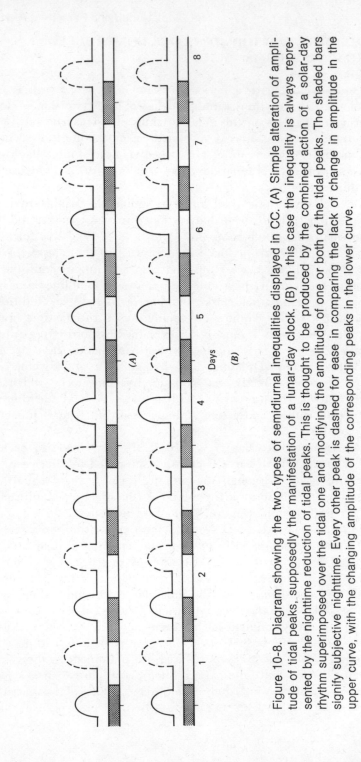

Figure 10-8. Diagram showing the two types of semidiurnal inequalities displayed in CC. (A) Simple alteration of amplitude of tidal peaks, supposedly the manifestation of a lunar-day clock. (B) In this case the inequality is always represented by the nighttime reduction of tidal peaks. This is thought to be produced by the combined action of a solar-day rhythm superimposed over the tidal one and modifying the amplitude of one or both of the tidal peaks. The shaded bars signify subjective nighttime. Every other peak is dashed for ease in comparing the lack of change in amplitude in the upper curve, with the changing amplitude of the corresponding peaks in the lower curve.

the same as portrayed in Figure 3-5, but where only partial, rather than complete, suppression of every other peak occurs).

In addition to amplitude alternation, the intervals between successive tidal peaks in organisms such as *Synchelidium* and *Excirolana* (Chapter 2) alternate in length; For example, during the first day in CC the interval between the great and small peaks may be longer than the interval between the small and great peaks. Since a vacillating period cannot be a property of a good clock, the results are again best explained by postulating control by a lunar-day clock.

As another line of evidence, it will be remembered that the period of the swimming rhythm in *Synchelidium* deviated more from the period displayed in nature, the longer the animal was maintained in CC. Instead of lengthening uniformly between peaks, the major increments occurred between every two peaks—again suggesting that the basic period is a *circalunadian* one. (I propose the circalunadian term to replace the often used terms *circatidal* and *circalunar*, the former being adequate but less precise if the basic period truly approximates the lunar day and the latter having been used in the literature to describe both lunar day and monthly rhythms.)

Finally, attention is drawn to the fact that only those organismic rhythms that match the basic periodicities produced by the movements of the earth, moon, and sun in relation to one another have all the characteristic properties of clock control. Tidal rhythms seem to have many of these properties, yet the tidal interval is not a primary cosmic period—only a hemiperiod of the lunar day. This again suggests that tidal rhythms should be considered as the overt expression of a lunar-day clock dictating a bimodal waveform pattern. At any rate, for the present, this will be the working hypothesis assumed.

A SEPARATE LUNAR-DAY CLOCK?

It is quite obvious that rhythms with a period of 24.8 h in nature or thereabouts, when moved to CC, are unique and not just simply a part of the spectrum of circadian frequencies longer than 24 h. Being distinct raises the question of whether they are driven by a specific lunar-day clock or whether a single clock (circadian, circalunadian, or possibly an intermediate frequency) drives both tidal and daily rhythms. The former possibility needs no further discussion; it attains the same hypothetical status as the circadian clock. The latter, more radical idea requires a qualifying frequency-transformation hypothesis and some supporting evidence.

Presumably, the clock driving tidal rhythms is coupled to them in a way similar to the connection between solar-day clocks and daily rhythms. Observations point to this; for example, as described in Chapter 8, it is possible with low-temperature pulses to produce what appears to be a temporary uncoupling between horologe and tidal locomotor activity in the green crab. Brief chilling of arrhythmic crabs (some devoid of rhythms since birth) instilled a tidal rhythm in them (Chapter 2); because the brief temperature pulse relayed no information on periodicity, the finding is best interpreted as a stimulus-forced coupling of an already running clock with the locomotory process. At any rate, by assuming the existence of a coupling transducer entity that also functions to transmute a clock frequency into circalunadian periods, a specific lunar-day clock is not needed. An organism provided with a single clock and solar- and lunar-day couplers would display both types of rhythms. Organisms that lacked one type of coupler would be less versatile. A simple mechanical model of this idea appears in Figure 10-9. In this elementary analogy it is obvious that the size of the belt-driven pulleys representing the coupling mechanisms alter the frequency information of the single clock sufficiently to produce different waveforms on the chart. Carrying this transmogrified model to the organism, the chart represents the overt rhythm, and the clock remains as it has for the last 50 years—an enigmatic postulate. The coupler also cannot as yet be identified, but we may be seeing some overt signs of its reality in the form of phase-response rhythms.

What evidence supports the idea that just a single clock is present? First, intuitively from an evolutionary point of view, it would have been

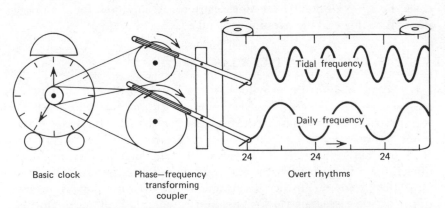

Basic clock   Phase—frequency   Overt rhythms
                     transforming
                     coupler

Figure 10-9. Physical analogue representation of the phase-frequency transforming coupler interposed between a "biological" clock and its overt "driven rhythms." Note that in this model the size of the belt-driven pulleys of the coupler determine the period of the rhythm charted. Thus, both tidal and daily rhythms are produced by the same clock (Palmer, 1973).

less "tedious" to develop a single clock rather than two separate ones whose periods differ by only slightly more than 3% (i.e., 51 min), especially when the organism is provided with at least two known phase-response mechanisms (and probably more) capable of adjusting the driven rhythm to a wide range of periods beleaguering both basic frequencies. The final evolutionary contrivance would be directly analogous to the wristwatches often worn by surf fishermen—timepieces whose single escapement frequency is transformed to time-of-day and time-of-tide expressions on the dial.

Secondly, of all the chemical substances used to try to alter circadian clockworks, only two—ethyl alcohol and deuterium oxide—have been found to have reproducible chronomutagenic effects. When a circalunadian rhythm was subjected to these substances (Enright, 1971a–b), it was found to be altered in the same way as circadian rhythms had been. This suggests the solar- and lunar-day clocks are either identical in makeup or are one and the same.

For partisans of the nonescapement hypothesis, a postulated single "receiving" clock fitted with daily and lunar-day frequency transforming couplers might seem to be unnecessary: If an organism is able to "read" solar-day rhythms in the subtle geophysical environment, why could it not also read the lunar-day ones? The reason could be that since the daily rhythms in these forces have amplitudes many fold greater than the lunar-day components, an organism would have to be just that many times more sensitive to the forces to respond to the lunar-day differences.

Finally, whether or not one clock serves both rhythms, certainly there is some kind of coupling between tidal and daily rhythms. Three lines of evidence dictate this fact.

First, LD cycles seem to have no direct entrainment effect on tidal rhythms unless a daily rhythmic component is also present in the process. When the latter condition obtains, the tidal rhythm is shifted in the same direction and approximate amount as the daily component by light-pulse and entrainment experiments—as was found with the fiddler crab color-change and activity rhythms (Chapter 7). This certainly indicates that the two rhythmic components are coupled together in some manner.

Second, while under LD 12:12 cycles, the fiddler crab activity rhythm was shown to display a strict 24.8-h bimodal interval. In CC the rhythm becomes circalunadian (compare Figure 2-7 with 2-8, and 2-10 with 2-11). The restriction of the period by LD suggests that the two rhythms are intimately conjoined.

Last, again with the fiddler crab activity rhythm, it was demonstrated that in CC the fine adjustment of the phase of the tidal peaks was a function of the hour of the solar day (Figure 2-10).

SUMMARY AND CONCLUSIONS

1. A discussion was conducted on the location of the clock within the organism, whether there is only one master clock per cell or a republic of many clocks, the clock's innateness, the means by which the clock is coupled to the process it forces to be rhythmic, the very important role of the phase-response rhythm in the entertainment of other rhythms to environmental cycles and the genesis of the circa- periods in CC, and the resistance of the period of rhythms to manipulation with chemicals.

2. The pros and cons of the two presently popular hypotheses concerning the nature of the clocks was reviewed and discussed.

3. An argument was constructed claiming that tidal rhythms are best thought of as bimodal lunar-day rhythms; that is, rhythms having a fundamental period of 24.8-h rather than the more usually expected tidal interval of 12.4-h. In CC, the period can deviate from 24.8-h, and then the rhythm is said to be *circalunadian*.

4. After speculating that a frequency transforming coupler may function between clock and overt rhythm, reasons were given that lead to the further speculation that both circadian and circalunadian rhythms could be generated by a single clock via a specific coupling mechanism.

5. Let me close by repeating the bromide that there is a great deal left to be learned about both circadian and circalunadian rhythms—especially the latter. It is hoped that some of the speculation offered here, set in the framework of what little is already known about tidal rhythmic behavior, will serve to stimulate further thought and experimental design. Whatever line individual investigators choose, the emphasis should be directed at finding new properties, which in turn may be used to decipher the clockworks. Because organismic rhythmicity is fundamental to essentially all life, the elucidation of the clock, or clocks, governing these rhythms will be one of the most important contributions made to biology.

Literature Cited

Andrews, R.V. 1967. Temporal secretory responses of cultured hamster adrenals. *Comp. Biochem. Physiol.*, 26:179–193.

Andrews, R.V., and G.E. Folk, Jr. 1963. Circadian metabolic patterns in cultured hamster adrenal glands. *Comp. Biochem. Physiol.*, 11:393–409.

Aschoff, J. 1960. Exogenous and endogenous components in circadian rhythms. *Cold Spring Harbor Symp. Quant. Biol.*, 25:11–28.

Aschoff, J. 1969. Desynchronization and resynchronization of human circadian rhythms. *Aerospace Med.*, 40:844–849.

Aschoff, J., U. Gerecke, and R. Wever. 1967. Desynchronization of human circadian rhythms. *Jap. Jour. Physiol.*, 17:450–457.

Aschoff, J., and J. Meyer-Lohmann. 1954. Angeborene 24-Studen-Periodik beim Kuecken. *Pflügers Arch.*, 260:170–176.

Ball, N.G., and G.B. Newcombe. 1961. The relationship between the growth of the primary leaf and of the coleoptile in seedlings of *Avena* and *Triticum*. *Jour. Exp. Bot.*, 12:114–128.

Barnett, A. 1965. A circadian rhythm of mating type reversals in *Paramecium multimicronucleatum*. In J. Aschoff, Ed., *Circadian Clocks*. North-Holland Publishing Co., Amsterdam, pp. 305–308.

Barnett, A. 1966. A circadian rhythm of mating type reversals in *Paramecium multimicronucleatum,* syngen 2, and its genetic control. *J. Cell. Physiol.,* 67:239–270.

Barnett, A. 1969. Cell division: a second circadian clock system in *Paramecium multimicronucleatum*. *Science,* 164:1417–1418.

Bennett, M.F. and J. Huguenin. 1969. Geomagnetic effects on a circadian difference in reaction times in earthworms. *Z. vergl. Physiol.,* 63:440–445.

Brady, J. 1969. How are insect circadian rhythms controlled? *Nature,* 223:781–784.

Brady, J. 1971. The search for an insect clock. In M. Menaker, Ed., *Biochronometry*. National Academy of Sciences, Washington, D.C., pp. 517–526.

Brown, F.A., Jr. 1960. Response to pervasive geophysical factors and the biological clock problem. *Cold Spring Harbor Symp. Quant. Biol.,* 25:57–71.

Brown, F.A., Jr. 1962a. Responses of the planarian, *Dugesia,* and the protozoan, *Paramecium,* to very weak horizontal magnetic fields. *Biol. Bull.,* 123:264–281.

Brown, F.A., Jr. 1962b. Response of the planarian, *Dugesia,* to very weak horizontal electrostatic fields. *Biol. Bull.,* 123:282–294.

Brown, F.A., Jr. 1971. Some orientational influences of non-visual terrestrial electromagnetic fields. *Ann. N.Y. Acad. Sci.,* 188:224–241.

Brown, F.A., Jr. 1972. The "clocks" timing biological rhythms. *Amer. Sci.,* 60:756–766.

Brown, F.A., Jr., M.F. Bennett, and C.L. Ralph. 1955. Apparent reversible influence of cosmic-ray-induced showers upon a biological system. *Proc. Soc. Exp. Biol. Med.,* 89:332–337.

Brown, F.A., Jr., and C.S. Chow. 1973. Interorganismic and environmental influences through extremely weak electromagnetic fields. *Biol. Bull.,* 144:437–461.

Brown, F.A., Jr., J.W. Hastings, and J.D. Palmer. 1970. *The Biological Clock: Two Views,* 2nd ed. Academic, New York.

Brown, F.A., Jr. and Y.H. Park. 1964. Seasonal variation in sign and strength of gamma-taxis in planarians. *Nature,* 202:469–471.

Brown, F.A., Jr. and Y.H. Park. 1965. Phase-shifting a lunar rhythm in planarians by altering the horizontal magnetic vector. *Biol. Bull.,* 128:79–86.

Brown, F.A., Jr., Y.H. Park, and J.R. Zeno. 1966. Diurnal variation in organismic response to very weak gamma radiation. *Nature,* 211:830–833.

Brown, F.A., Jr. and H.M. Webb. 1968. Some temporal and geographic relations of snail response to vary weak gamma radiation. *Physiol. Zool.,* 41:385–400.

Bruce, V.G. 1972. Mutants of the biological clock in *Chlamydomonas reinhardi. Genetics,* 70:537–548.

Bruce, V.G., and C.S. Pittendrigh. 1960. An effect of heavy water on the phase and period of the circadian rhythm in *Euglena. J. Cell. Comp. Physiol.,* 56:25–31.

Bryant, T.R. 1972. Gas exchange in dry seeds: circadian rhythmicity in the absence of DNA replication, transcription, and translation. *Science,* 178:634–636.

Bünning, E. 1935a. Zur Kenntnis der endogenen Tagesrhythmik bei Insekten und Pflanzen. *Ber. deutsch. bot. Ges.,* 53:594–623.

Bünning, E. 1935b. Zur Kenntnis der erblichen Tagesperiodizität bei den Primärblättern von *Phaseolus multiflorus. Jahrb. Wiss. Bot.,* 81:411–418.

Bünning, E. 1958. Das Weiterlaufen der "Physiologischen Uhr" im Säugerdarm ohne zentrale Steuervng. *Naturwiss.,* 45:68.

Bünning, E., and J. Baltes. 1963. Zur Wirkung von schweren Wasser auf die endogene Tagesrhythmik. *Naturwiss.,* 50:622.

Clayton, D.L., and J.V. Paietta. 1972. Selection for circadian eclosion time in *Drosphila melanogaster. Science,* 178:994–995.

Conroy, R.T., and J.N. Mills. 1970. *Human Circadian Rhythms.* Churchill, London.

De Coursey, P.J. 1961. Effect of light on the circadian activity rhythm of the flying squirrel *Glaucomys volans. Z. vergl. Physiol.,* 44:331–354.

De Coursey, P.J. 1964. Function of a light response rhythm in hamsters. *Cell. Comp. Physiol.,* 63:189–196.

Dowse, H.B., and J.D. Palmer. 1969. Entrainment of circadian activity rhythms in mice by electrostatic fields. *Nature,* 222:564–566.

Dowse, H.B., and J.D. Palmer. 1972. The chronomutagenic effect of deuterium oxide on the period and entrainment of a biological rhythm. *Biol. Bull.,* 143:513–524.

Enderle, W. 1951. Tagesperiodische Wachstums- und Turgorschwankungen an Gewebekulturen. *Planta,* 39:570–588.

Enright, J.T. 1963. Endogenous tidal and lunar rhythms. *Proc. XVI. Inter. Cong. Zool.,* 4:355–359.

Enright, J.T. 1971a. Heavy water slows biological timing processes. *Z. vergl. Physiol.*, 72:1–16.

Enright, J.T. 1971b. The internal clock of drunken isopods. *Z. vergl. Physiol.*, 75:332–346.

Feldman, J. 1967. Lengthening the period of a biological clock in *Euglena* by cycloheximide, an inhibitor of protein synthesis. *Proc. Nat. Acad. Sci.*, 57:1080–1087.

Harker, J.E. 1954. Diurnal rhythm in *Periplaneta americana* L. *Nature*, 173:689–690.

Harker, J.E. 1956. Factors controlling the diurnal rhythms of activity of *Periplaneta americana*, L. *J. Exp. Biol.*, 33:224–234.

Hastings, J.W., and B.M. Sweeney. 1958. A persistent diurnal rhythm of luminescence in *Gonyaulax polyedra. Biol. Bull.*, 115:440–458.

Hoffmann, K. 1957. Angeborene Tagesperiodik bei Eidechsen. *Naturwiss.*, 44:359–360.

Hoffmann, K. 1960. Experimental manipulation of the orientational clock in birds. *Cold Spring Harbor Symp. Quant. Biol.*, 25:379–387.

Jacklet, J.W. 1969. Circadian rhythm of optic nerve impulses recorded in darkness from isolated eye of *Aplysia. Science*, 164:562–563.

Keeton, W.T. 1971. Magnets interfere with pigeon homing. *Proc. Nat. Acad. Sci.*, 68:102–106.

Keller, S. 1960. Über die Wirkung chemischer Faktoren auf die tagesperiodischen Blattbewegungen von *Phaseolus multiflorus. Z. Bot.*, 48:32–57.

Konopka, R.J., and S. Benzer. 1971. Clock mutants of *Drosophila melanogaster. Proc. Nat. Acad. Sci.*, 68:2112–2116.

Lobban, M.C. 1965. Dissociation in human rhythmic functions. In J. Aschoff, Ed., *Circadian Clocks.* North-Holland Publishing Co., Amsterdam, pp. 219–227.

McMurry, L., and J.W. Hastings. 1972. No desynchronization among four circadian rhythms in the unicellular alga, *Gonyaulax polyedra. Science,* 175:1137–1138.

Moser, I. 1962. Phasenverschiebungen der endogenen Tagesrhythmik bei *Phaseolus* durch Temperatur- und Lichtintensitätsänderungen. *Planta,* 58:199–219.

Ogata, N., M. Nishi, and T. Yabe. 1955. Diurnal fluctuation in the rate of bacteria multiplication. *Yokohoma Med. Bull.*, 6:67–71.

Overland, L. 1960. Endogenous rhythm in the opening and odor of flowers of *Cestrum nocturnum. Amer. Jour. Bot.*, 47:375–382.

Palmer, J.D. 1963. Organismic spatial orientation in very weak magnetic fields. *Nature*, 198:1061–1062.

Palmer, J.D. 1964. Comparative studies in avian persistent rhythms: spontaneous change in period length. *Comp. Biochem. Physiol.*, 21:273–282.

Palmer, J.D. 1973. Tidal rhythms: the clock control of the rhythmic physiology of marine organisms. *Biol. Rev.*, 48:377–418.

Palmer, J.D., and H.B. Dowse. 1969. Preliminary findings on the effect of D_2O on the period of circadian activity rhythms. *Biol. Bull.*, 137:388.

Pittendrigh, C. 1961. On temporal organization in living systems. In *The Harvey Lectures.* Academic, New York, pp. 93–125.

Pittendrigh, C.S. 1965. On the mechanism of the entrainment of a circadian rhythm by light cycles. In J. Aschoff, Ed., *Circadian Clocks.* North-Holland Publishing Co., Amsterdam, pp. 276–297.

Pittendrigh, C.S. 1967. Circadian systems. I. The driving oscillation and its assay in *Drosophila pseudoobscura. Proc. Nat. Acad. Sci.*, 58:1762–1767.

Rogers, L., and G. Greenbank. 1930. The intermittent growth of bacterial cultures. *J. Bact.*, 19:181–190.

Rummel, J., E. Sallin, and H. Lipscomb. 1966. Circadian rhythms in simulated and manned orbital space flight. *Rass. Neurol. Veg.*, 21:41–56.

Sargent, M. L. 1969. Effects of four antibiotics on growth and periodicity of a rhythmic strain of *Neurospora. Neurospora Newsl.*, 15:17.

Schweiger, E., H.G. Wallraff, and H.G. Schweiger. 1964. Endogenous circadian rhythm in cytoplasm of *Acetabularia:* influence of the nucleus. *Science,* 146:658–659.

Semon, R. 1908. Hat der Rhythmus der Tageszeiten bei Pflanzen erbliche Eindrücke hinterlassen? *Biol. Central.*, 28:225–243.

Stadler, D.R. 1959. Genetic control of a cyclic growth pattern in *Neurospora. Nature,* 184:170–171.

Stephens, G.C. 1957. Influence of temperature fluctuations on the diurnal melanophore rhythm of the fiddler crab, *Uca. Physiol. Zool.*, 30:55–69.

Strumwasser, F. 1965. The demonstration and manipulation of a circadian rhythm in a single neuron. In J. Aschoff, Ed., *Circadian Clocks.* North-Holland Publishing Co., Amsterdam, pp. 442–462.

Sussman, A., R. Lowry, and T. Durkee. 1964. Morphology and genetics of a periodic colonial mutant of *Neurospora crassa. Amer. J. Bot.*, 51:243–252.

Suter, R.B., and K.S. Rawson. 1968. Circadian activity rhythm of the deer mouse, *Peromyscus:* effect of deuterium oxide. *Science,* 160:1011–1014.

Sweeney, B.M. 1960. The photosynthetic rhythm in single cells of

Gonyaulax polyedra. Cold Spring Harbor Symp. Quant. Biol., 25: 145–148.

Sweeney, B.M. 1963. Biological clocks in plants. *Ann. Rev. Plant Physiol.,* 14:411–440.

Sweeney, B.M., and F.T. Haxo. 1961. Persistence of a photosynthetic rhythm in enucleated *Acetabularia. Science,* 134:1361–1363.

Tharp, G.D., and G.E. Folk. 1964. Rhythmic changes in rate of the mammalian heart and heart cells during prolonged isolation. *Comp. Biochem. Physiol.,* 14:255–273.

Truman, J.W. 1971. The role of the brain in the ecdysis rhythm of silkmoths: comparison with the photoperiodic termination of diapause. In M. Menaker, Ed., *Biochronometry.* National Academy of Sciences, Washington, D.C., pp. 483–504.

Wever, R. 1967. Über die Beeinflussung der circadianen Periodik des Menschen durch schwache elektromagnetische Felder. *Z. vergl. Physiol.,* 56:111–128.

Wever, R. 1969. Gesetzmässigkeiten der circadianen Periodik des Menschen, geprüft an der Wirkung eines schwachen elektrischen Wechselfeldes. *Pflügers Arch.,* 302:97–122.

Wilkins, M.B. 1959. An endogenous rhythm in the rate of CO_2 output of *Bryophyllum.* I. Some preliminary experiments. *J. Exp. Bot.,* 10:377–390.

Wiltschko, W., and R. Wiltschko. 1972. Magnetic compass of European robins. *Science,* 176:62–64.

Zimmer, R. 1962. Phasenverschiebung und andere Störlichtwirkungen auf die endogen tagesperiodischen Blütenblattbewegungen von *Kalanchoë bossfeldiana. Planta,* 58:283–300.

Zimmerman, W.F., C.S. Pittendrigh, and T. Pavlidis. 1968. Temperature compensation of the circadian oscillation in *Drosophila pseudoobscura* and its entrainment by temperature cycles. *J. Insect Physiol.,* 14:669–684.

Glossary

Amplitude—A measurement of the height of the peaks relative to troughs of a cycle (which see):

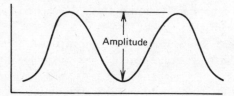

Biological clock—The mechanism that is thought to time those organismic rhythms that persist in LL and TT. The clock has not yet been identified, but the properties thus far elucidated lead to two hypothetical clockwork schemes: the escapement- and nonescapement-type living clocks (which see).

Biological horologe—A living clock (see "Biological clock").

CC—Abbreviation for *constant conditions* (which see).

Chronomutagenic agent—(*Chrono* = time; *mutatio* = change; *genic* = producing). Any substance that produces an alteration in the phase or period of a biological rhythm.

Circadian rhythm—(*circa* = about; *diem* = day). Rhythms about a day in length. Used formally, as it is in this book, it stands for solar-day rhythms that persist in CC with a slight deviation from the 24-h period displayed in nature (Figure 1-5).

Circalunadian—A basic lunar-day rhythm—almost always bimodal—that persists in CC with a period either slightly longer or shorter than 24.8-h (Figure 1-4).

Circamonthly rhythm—A persistent synodic monthly rhythm whose period differs slightly from 29.5 days.

Circannual rhythm—A persistent annual rhythm whose period differs somewhat from 365 days.

Circatidal rhythm—A basic tidal rhythm that persists in CC with a period deviating slightly from 12.4-h (Figure 1-4).

Constant conditions—A laboratory setting in which at least the levels of illumination and temperature do not vary.

Cycle—A sequence of events through time that repeat themselves in the same order and at the same interval:

DD—Abbreviation for *constant darkness.*

Diurnal solar-day rhythm—One in which the major peak(s) comes during the hours of light.

Entraining agent—Same as *zeitgeber* (which see).

Escapement clock—Any clock, such as a wristwatch, grandfather, or cesium clock, that generates its own interval of time autonomously.

Form—The shape of the curve describing a cycle.

Fortnightly interval—One-half of a synodic month: 14.75 days.

Free-running period—The same as *natural period* (which see).

Frequency—The number of cycles per unit time; the inverse of the period.

LD—Abbreviation for light–dark cycle. The notation is often followed by a numerical ratio indicating the duration in hours of illumination and darkness (in that order) and a parenthetic statement as to the intensity of the light used. For example, LD 8:16 (12 ft-c) signifies a light–dark cycle of 8-h of light whose intensity is 12 ft-c alternating with 16-h of darkness. Sometimes in lieu of a light intensity or duration, *nat.* is used, signifying natural illumination such as might enter through a laboratory window, or that encountered in the habitat.

LL—Abbreviation for *constant light;* that is, a laboratory situation where the intensity of illumination is held constant.

Lunar day—The 24-h, 51-min interval between consecutive moonrises; one rotation of the earth in relation to the moon (Figure 1-6).

Natural period—The fundamental period of a clock when it is not entrained to some forcing oscillation.

Neap tides—those tides occurring twice each month in which the magnitude of exchange is smallest; that is, times of the highest lows and lowest high tides (Figure 1-8B; 1-9).

Nocturnal solar-day rhythm—One in which the major peak(s) come during the hours of darkness.

Nonescapement clock—Any clock, such as a sundial or electric clock, that does not generate its own interval of time, but instead simply signals an interval relayed to it from some outside source (e.g., in keeping with the above samples, the passage of the sun overhead or the 60-cycle alternating line current).

Oscillation—In this book, same as *cycle* (which see).

Period—The time interval of one complete cycle:

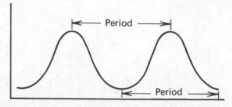

Periodic—In this book, same as *cyclic* (which see).

Persistent rhythm—Any organismic rhythm that will continue to be displayed in CC.

Phase—Some arbitrarily chosen fraction of a cycle; for example, four obvious phases exist in a single cycle:

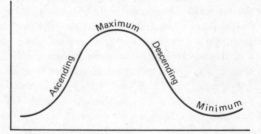

It is also a relative term used to describe where a particular phase of one cycle is in relation to another; for example, "the activity phase of the crab's rhythm is in phase with the flood tide" or "Green crabs run at high tide and fiddler crabs at ebb—the animals are about 6-h out of phase with one another."

Phase angle—A relative term measuring in "degrees" (or sometimes in units of time) the distance between a particular point in a cycle and some arbitrarily chosen constant reference point. For example, if a natural diurnal rhythm (which see) is subjected to reversed LD cycles in the laboratory, the rhythm inverts and is then said to be 180° out of phase with the old natural LD cycle. Or, if the moment of "light on" in an LD cycle is arbitrarily given a value of 0, if the 24-h period of a rhythm is divided into 360° (a permissible practice, since oscillations are linear projections of circular motion), and if the major peak of the rhythm comes 6-h after the dark-to-light transition, the phase angle is 90°.

Phase-response rhythm (curve)—A waveform plot describing the direction and amount of phase change produced in a rhythm subjected to an appropriate phase-change-producing stimulus (Figures 8-1; 10-2).

Rhythm—Used here to signify any organismic process or behavior pattern that is cyclic (see Cycle).

Semidiurnal inequality—A condition found on many coastlines, in which the two tidal innundations on any one lunar day are of unequal amplitude, one being higher than the other (Figures 1-7; 1-9). In some cases, organisms collected from a shoreline subjected to this inequality in tidal amplitude display the characteristic in their persistent rhythms (Figures 2-16; 2-18).

Solar day—The 24-h interval between consecutive sunrises. One rotation of the earth in relation to the sun.

Spring tides—Those tides occurring twice each month in which the magnitude of exchange is greatest; that is, the times of the highest highs and the lowest low tides (Figures 1-8A; 1-9).

Subjective day—That span of hours in CC that had been daytime for the experimental organism before being placed in CC.

Subjective night—That span of hours in CC that had been nighttime for the experimental organism before being placed in CC.

Synodic month—The 29.5-day interval between consecutive new moons.

Transients—In some organisms, after exposure to a single pulse of light or temperature in otherwise CC, one or more intermediate phase angles are displayed before the final steady-state phase is adopted The intermediate angles are termed *transients.*

TT—Abbreviation for *constant temperature.*

Zeitgeber—Time-giver; any external stimulus that will entrain or rephase a biological rhythm.

Acknowledgments

Figure 1-2. Reproduced by permission of the National Research Council of Canada from the *Canadian Journal of Botany*. **47**: 287–298 (1969).

Figure 1-3. Reprinted by permission of *Natural History* magazine, March, 1966. Copyright © The American Museum of Natural History, 1966.

Figure 1-5, 5-1, 9-10. Taken from: Brown et al. 1970. *The Biological Clock: Two Views*. Courtesy of Academic Press, N. Y.

Figures 2-3, 2-7, 2-8, 2-9, 2-10, 2-11, 2-18, 2-21, 3-3, 3-4, 9-8, 9-13, 10-5, 10-6. Reprinted with permission of *Biological Bulletin*.

Figure 2-4. Reprinted with permission of the *Journal of Theoretical Biology*.

Figures 2-13, 2-14, 2-15, 5-4, 5-5, 7-1, 7-8, 8-2, 8-6, 8-7, 8-8. Reprinted with permission of the *Journal of Experimental Biology*.

Figure 2-22. Taken from: Gibson, R. 1967. Experiments on the tidal rhythm of *Blennius Pholis*. *J. mar. biol. Ass. U. K.* **47**: 97–111. Courtesy of Cambridge University Press.

Figure 3-1. Taken from: Keeble, F. 1910. *Plant-animals: A Study in Symbiosis*. Courtesy of Cambridge University Press.

Figure 3-2. Taken from: Palmer, J., and F. Round. 1965. Persistent, vertical-migration rhythms in Benthic Microflora. I. The effect of light and temperature on the rhythmic behavior of *Euglena Obtusa*. *J. mar. biol. Ass. U. K.* **45**: 567–582. Courtesy of Cambridge University Press.

Figure 3-6. Taken from: Harris, J. 1963. The role of endogenous rhythms in vertical migration. *J. mar. biol. Ass. U. K.* **43**: 153–166. Courtesy of Cambridge University Press.

Figure 5-3, 6-1. Reprinted with permission of the *American Journal of Physiology*.

Figure 7-2. Taken from: Enright, J. 1965. Entrainment of a tidal rhythm. *Science,* **147**: 864–867. Courtesy of American Association for the Advancement of Science.

Figures 7-6, 7-7. Taken from: Naylor, E. and F. Atkinson. 1972. Pressure and the rhythmic behavior of inshore marine animals. In: *The Effects of Pressure on Organisms*. (Eds. M. Sleigh and G. Alister), pp. 395–415. Courtesy of Academic Press.

Figure 8-1. Taken from: Zimmerman, W., C. Pittendrigh, and T. Paulidis. 1968. Temperature compensation of the circadian oscillation in *Drosophila Pseudoobscura* and its entrainment by temperature cycles. *J. Insect Physiol.,* **14**: 669–684. Courtesy of Pergamon Publ. Co.

Figure 8-4. Taken from: Brown, F. and H. Webb. 1948. Temperature relations of an endogenous daily rhythmicity in the fiddler crab, *Uca. Physiol. Zool.*, **21**: 371–381. Courtesy of the University of Chicago Press.

Figure 8-5. Taken from: Stephens, G. 1957. Influence of temperature fluctuations on the diurnal melanophore rhythm of the fiddler crab, *Uca. Physiol. Zool.*, **30**: 55–69. Courtesy of the University of Chicago Press.

Figure 9-4. Taken from: Pardi, L. 1960. Innate components in the solar orientation of littoral amphipods. *Cold Spring Harbor Symp. Quant. Biol.*, **25**: 395–401. Courtesy of Cold Spring Harbor Laboratory.

Figure 9-5. Reprinted with permission of *Botanica Marina*. Figure appeared in Vol. 4, page 150, 1962.

Figures 9-7, 10-2. Taken from Aschoff, J. (Ed.). 1965. *Circadian Clocks*. Courtesy North-Holland Publ. Co.

Figure 9-14. Reprinted by permission from *Natural History* magazine, April, 1970. Copyright © The American Museum of Natural History, 1970.

Subject Index